History of

Wine Words

Also By Charles Hodgson

Global Wording
The Fascinating Story of the Evolution of English

An audio book from Macmillan Audio, New York
available online and on CD
www.globalwording.com

Carnal Knowledge
A Navel Gazer's Dictionary of Anatomy, Etymology, and Trivia

A book about the words we use for our bodies.

From St. Martin's Press, New York
www.navelgazersdictionary.com

Podictionary
The Podcast for Word Lovers

Every day, a surprising history of a word you thought you knew.

Read or listen online or on your iPod.
www.podictionary.com

History of

Wine Words

An Intoxicating Dictionary

of

Etymology and Word Histories

from

the Vineyard, Glass, and Bottle

Charles Hodgson

P2Peak Press
www.p2peak.com

Library and Archives Canada Cataloguing in Publication

Hodgson, Charles, 1958-
    History of wine words : an intoxicating dictionary of etymology and word histories from the vineyard, glass, and bottle / Charles Hodgson.

Includes index.
ISBN 978-0-9811224-0-3

    1. Wine and wine making--Dictionaries.
2. Viticulture--Dictionaries. I. Title.

TP546.H69 2009   641.2'2014   C2009-901322-3

Additional suggested Library of Congress Subject Headings:
    Wine--Social Aspects.
    Language and culture.
    English language--Etymology.
    Wine districts.
    Wine labels.
    English language--History.
    Wine--History.
    Wine grapes.

1.0

For Ella,
old wine to drink, old friend to trust

As olde wood is best to burne; old horse to ride; old books to reade; and old wine to drinke; so are old friends alwayes most trusty to vse.

Leonard Wright, 1594

Contents

Acknowledgements

As I was writing this book, I would post daily entries on a blog where I had invited a group of volunteer readers to follow along. They deserve thanks for enduring my unedited prose and more so for their suggestions and guidance.

So often there are more people to thank than space allows. Fortunately, in this case, space *does* allow me to thank these supportive souls individually. So, in alphabetical order, then: Thank you Johanne Blais, Bob Campbell, John Fischer, David Lawrason, Anatoly Liberman, Tim Patterson, Rod Phillips, Jancis Robinson, Joe Rouse, Mark Tandan, Debbie Trenholm, José Vouillamoz, and Tom Wark. Thanks also to my editor, Laura Byrne Paquet, and to Nicolas Pin of Snowy Day Design for the cover. I raise a glass to each one of you.

That said, we can be sure that this book contains errors and inaccuracies. What book doesn't? My apologies in advance for these; the fault is mine. Please send your corrections and suggestions to winewordsuggestion@gmail.com

Introduction

The book you hold in your hands is a little like a mixed case of wine in that it represents a selection. There are words about reds and whites, as well as samples from different vineyards and different countries. Like the offerings at a wine tasting, they are selections from a vastly larger list of possibilities, chosen to show off particular attributes. Unlike wines, there aren't "good" and "bad" words; a writer doesn't get paid more for using *champagne* than for using *plonk* in a sentence. But just like wines, words have their individual characters.

Let me explain what you might want to look for in a word. Instead of the bouquet, the rim color or the length of finish on the palate that you might appreciate in a wine, in these wine words I'd like you to look for the personalities of the words.

"How can a word have a personality?" you ask. You might as well ask, "How can a wine?" The words in this book come from different parent languages and carry their heritage with them. Some of the words are the names of places where wine is produced. Others are the names of grape varieties or relate to the way wine is grown and made. Some of the words included may not seem to have anything at all to do with wine, but you will be pleasantly surprised once you pull the etymological cork.

Words have a heritage. You've likely heard that many English words are based on Latin. For the words in a book about wine words, that is doubly true. French, a Romance language, had a big influence on our English wine vocabulary, as well as a bigger, older influence on English itself, starting about 1000 years ago. So when you find a wine word that *doesn't* have a Latin etymology, savor it. Deeper than Latin are

Indo-European language roots. They go about as far back as wine does in our cultural heritage—more than 5000 years, and maybe as far as 8000 or 9000.

Look for words that denote locations or grape varieties. Some of both of these types of names have arisen recently and their origins can be certified. Other names are ancient and their roots almost beyond telling. That is the nature of etymology: sometimes there is a solid paper trail, but at other times determining a word's root is simply guesswork (but, with the right source material, educated guesswork).

In choosing entries that have to do with locations—such as Bordeaux or Napa—I've tried to anticipate the names readers might recognize. The book doesn't cover the entire map; the number of châteaux alone would be impossible to fit into this volume. Similarly, there are hundreds and hundreds of grape variety names, but the majority of us wouldn't recognize most of them.

Words that appear on their surface to have nothing to do with wine are often really a reflection of the fact that wine has played a bigger part in the development of Western society than most of us appreciate. For the last few thousand years, people have been investing a lot of money and effort in producing and consuming wine, so it's no wonder that some of the technical language they used in their work snuck into the building blocks that have been assembled into Modern English.

The range of words included is also representative of the mutability of words. Over time words change; pronunciation and spelling change, and so does meaning. Changes in meaning can happen over a few short years or a word can remain steadfast in its meaning for millennia. I find it particularly interesting to consider what it is about a word that allows it to resist or be transformed by the forces of change.

If you enjoy the book, please don't stop there. Visit the book's website (www.wine-words.com), where news will be posted of a wine words database and video-cast series now in the planning stages.

Wine Words

A

ABRUZZO • This Italian wine district is named for the Abruzzi Mountains. The mountains in turn may have been named from either the Latin word *apri* (meaning "boar") or *abruptus* (meaning "steep"), although neither of these sources is certain.

ACIDITY • One of the first appearances of the word *acidity* in English came in 1620 in reference to oranges, of which there were said to be two types. Sweet oranges were said to "subvert the appetite and cause loathsomeness in the stomach," while sour oranges quenched thirst, excited appetite, and repressed vomiting. Sugar was recommended to "correct their acidity." This citation comes from a document entitled *Via recta ad vitam longam*, which is Latin for "the straight road to long life." Among other things, the work discussed food and drink as they were thought to affect health. Oranges rated only a short section therein but, because wine was seen as so healthful and yet so fraught with danger, about 7 percent of the book was dedicated to wine, amounting to almost 5000 words. The author explains that wine is "the most pleasant liquour of all other, and was made from the beginning to exhilarate the heart of man." Yet he warns that children should not be given wine due to the fact that it fills their heads with vapors. He also decries the belief then current that getting sloshed once or twice a month promoted health, saying, "the hurt is farre greater then the helpe." *Acidity's* parent word *acid* didn't appear in English until 1626 and both words had pre-existed in French and in Latin before that. The Latin root *accre* meant "to be sour" and in turn had deeper roots in the Indo-European word *ak*, meaning "sharp" or "pointed."

ADELAIDE • A centre of Australian wine education neighboring several winegrowing areas, the city of Adelaide

3

was named in 1836 at the request of King William IV of England to commemorate his queen. Queen Adelaide seems to have deserved the honor, having had to put up with marrying William in the first place: he was 50, she 25; he already had 10 illegitimate children; he liked the look of her simply because she might produce babies who'd be legitimate heirs to the throne if he became king; she went along with it and he did become king, yet all of her babies died. Against all odds, they seem to have been very happy together.

AFRICA • South Africa is the continent's most important wine nation. The name of the continent originated at its other end, in Tunisia on the southern shore of the Mediterranean. It's suspected that the local desert conditions influenced the naming of the inhabitants as "people of the desert." The Arabic word *afar*, meaning "dust" or "earth," stood in for "desert" and formed the root that became *Africa* and spread to the whole continent.

AGING • In the movie *The Jerk*, Steve Martin shows his lack of sophistication by telling a waiter he doesn't want any more of this *old* stuff, he wants some *fresh* wine. These days, dusty old bottles from prized vintages command huge prices, but before the 1700s it was the unsophisticated who would buy old wine. For centuries, wine was shipped and stored in wooden barrels. Glass bottles only became common in the 1600s, and even then wine made its journey from vintner to customer in barrels prone to oxygenation that promoted wine spoilage. For these reasons, wine prices were at their highest when new shipments first arrived and declined precipitously when next year's vintage became available. The introduction of bottles changed all that, and aging changed the bottle too. At first, bottles were bulbous and hard to stack. Once it was clear that wine improved in the bottle, it became obvious that cylindrical bottles that could be piled safely together were far more practical. The word *age* came to English from French and from Latin before that. Related words appeared in Greek and Germanic, but the most solid etymological tracings come from *aevum*, a Latin word meaning "lifetime." The meaning of the word was less "how old you are" and more "length of existence." Hence such expressions as "the age of the dinosaurs." (See **bottle**, p. 26.)

ALCOHOL • Kohl is a dark powder used as makeup in some cultures, and it shares an etymological connection to the active ingredient in wine and other alcoholic drinks. So strong is this etymological link that the earliest use of the word *alcohol* in English didn't refer to the flammable fluid but instead to the powdered makeup. Kohl was manufactured through a process that applied heat; in Arabic, the products of this and similar processes became known as *kuhl*. The Arabic word for "the" is *al*, so *al-kuhl* meant "the product of a heating process." In distillation, of course, a dilute product of fermentation is heated to produce alcohol. So it made perfect sense for those ancient Arabs to use the same word.

ALEXANDER VALLEY • This California wine region represents the largest area of Sonoma under vines and takes its name from Cyrus Alexander, who arrived there in the 1830s. Cyrus Alexander had been born in Pennsylvania and had already failed as a miner and a fur trapper before signing on with a San Diego financier and acting as his agent to establish a cattle operation. Geographical features are not usually named after failed miners, fur trappers, or cattle ranchers, so it would be correct to assume that the cattle endeavor was successful.

ALIGOTÉ • The grape type Aligoté was first reported in an English publication in 1912 but had appeared in 1807 in French. That first French writer was evidently unimpressed by the grape, since the citation reads, in translation: "aligoté...this plant is to destroy rather than build." Opinions must have changed by the time the word reached English, since that first citation in *The Oxford English Dictionary* claims that "the best wines of all are called Aligote, and the second-best—still very good—are called Pinot." But as the *OED* citations go on, the reputation of Aligoté suffers, until in 1958 *Spectator* magazine reports Aligoté to be the "cheapest and least fragile of white burgundies." The French name for this grape may have only just stabilized in spelling before making the jump to English. It appeared in 1866 as *alligotet* and is believed to have come from an Old French word, *harigoter*, that meant "to rip" or "to tear," which came from the Germanic parent *hariôn* with the same meaning. This etymology is by no means certain. However, assuming that it is accurate, there might be two opposing reasons why a vine might be given a name with a destructive meaning. The initial French citation supports the suggestion that vintners felt the vine deserved removal. An alternative origin might be that poor soil needed breaking up in order to plant the vines.

ALOXE-CORTON • Aloxe-Corton is a village in Burgundy mentioned as being a wine-producing area as early as the year 696. The *Dictionnaire étymologique des noms de lieux en France* agrees with Adrian Room's *Placenames of France* as to the origin of *Aloxe*, indicating that it may stem from *Alussius*, a Gaulish personal name. Corton was originally a separate place, but its name is also a grand cru appellation and is claimed by some to be a contraction of *Curtis Othonis*. *Curtis* comes from a Latin root meaning "enclosure." *Othonis* is said to refer to the Roman emperor Otho. The claim is thus that a local vineyard belonged to Emperor Otho. Yet Otho was only emperor for about three months in the year 69 and it seems unlikely that his name would have had such tenacity.

ALSACE • The dogs we know as *German shepherds* are also sometimes known as *Alsatians*. The reason for this is that, during World War I, English-speaking dog fanciers turned away from these innocent canine victims of guilt by association. Dog breeders came up with the idea of renaming the canines Alsatian wolf dogs for marketing purposes. Alsace is now French territory, but for the longest time it was German. Its German name is *Elssas*. The etymology of *Alsace* is uncertain, but there are several theories. *The Oxford English Dictionary* indicates that it is a Latin form of *El-sasz*, meaning "foreign settlement," but other theories include the idea that the mountains in the region inspired the name; the Gaulish word for "cliff" was *ailsa*. Another Gaulish source might be their word for a species of tree common there; alders were known as *aliso*. Yet another theory is that the area is named for the Ill River, which is reported to have earlier borne the name *Illzas*.

ALTO ADIGE • This Italian wine region is named for the Adige River, which was known to the Romans as *Atesis*. That name is thought to have evolved from the Indo-European root *at*, meaning "rapid," and to have been applied because of the river's swift current in its mountain descent. The word *alto* is Italian for "high" and comes from the Latin *altus*, which also gave English the ending of the word *exalt*.

AMADOR COUNTY • A California wine region in the Sierra Foothills east of Napa, this area was named after José María Amador. Born in San Francisco and serving militarily in the San Francisco Company, he was granted land in 1834; his name appeared on maps by 1844.

AMERICA • *Brewer's Dictionary of Phrase and Fable* says that *America* is a misnomer because the continents are named after someone who didn't actually do the discovering. Of course, there have been people in the Americas for thousands of years, and we know that Vikings also put in an appearance. However, America is named for Amerigo Vespucci, an Italian who sailed along the coast of South America in 1501. Christopher Columbus supposedly bumped into the Americas nine years earlier, so we might well have been calling the place *Christophica*. It was a German mapmaker in

1507 who suggested that these lands might actually be a whole new continent (or two) and called them *Americanus*. This spelling was due to the fashion in those days for writing scholarly things in Latin. The Italian name *Amerigo* is thought to be of Germanic origin, a name that translates literally as "work ruler" or more figuratively as "shop foreman."

AMETHYST • An amethyst is a grapey purple gemstone named for its color. The word *amethyst* came to English from Greek, via French and Latin. That's as far back as we can trace the word, but the tradition surrounding the word may well go back even further. The Greek etymology of *amethyst* gives it a meaning of "not intoxicating." The fact that red wine usually starts out pretty purple is the connection with the stone. The ancients figured that since the stone was the same color as wine, it must have some magical affiliation with wine. They associated all sorts of convenient attributes with the stone. Drinking vessels made from amethysts or decorated with amethysts let you enjoy yourself without the embarrassment of stumbling on your toga or being sick behind your host's marble statuary. Wives liked to have a few amethysts around because, even when their husbands went out on a tear, the amethysts stopped the wine from suppressing their inhibitions and thus prevented affairs. These hopeful notions make it particularly appropriate that this word first appeared in English in a document dedicated to an imaginary land of pleasure. Our source is a poem written circa 1290 called *The Land of Cokaygne*. Cokaygne in the Middle Ages was a mythical place where everything was easy. Geese flew already roasted into your mouth and pigs walked around already cooked, with a convenient carving knife protruding so you could slice off some lunch. It also rained pies. With all that good eating, you'd want a little good drinking too. That's when it was handy to have some amethysts around.

AMPELOGRAPHY • An ampelographer studies and documents the thousands of diverse grapevines. English got *ampelography* from French in 1879, but just barely, since even the fattest dictionaries usually omit the word unless they specialize in things enological. *Ampelography* is built on the Greek words *ampelos* (meaning "vine") and *graphia* (meaning "writing").

AMPHORA • An amphora is one of those huge clay bottles or jars with two handles at the top that you see in museums. Whether wine was invented or discovered, archeological evidence of its antiquity is contained in part in amphorae. It is thought that the region known as the *Fertile Crescent* was the birthplace of not only agriculture and civilization but of the wine industry as well. Based on the number and distribution of old amphorae finds, the word *industry* is not too strong a term. Not only are remnants of grape seeds, skins and tannins found in old amphorae—proving their use—but, because these vessels were made in different styles and with differing materials in different places, archaeologists can map the ancient wine trade by tracking the locations where amphorae were found. There is a practical reason for their name. The wine and amphora combined weighed in at well over 100 pounds. The shape of amphorae and the handles on top enabled two people to carry them, one person on each side. In Greek, *amphi* means "on two sides" and *pherein* means "to carry," so *amphora* literally means "carried from both sides." *Amphi* also shows up in our word *amphitheater*, a theater where the seats are arranged not facing the stage from just one side but in a full circle—figuratively, "both sides." With respect to the Greek word *pherein*, to "carry" something is to "bear" it, and it's no coincidence that the Greek *pherein* sounds a little like *bear*; they both come from the same Indo-European root word.

ANDERSON VALLEY • In Mendocino County, California, Anderson Valley was named for Walter Anderson, who is

9

said to have "discovered" it while out hunting at the beginning of the 1850s. Anderson's family name derives from "son of Andrew" and *Andrew* in turn from the Greek *Andreas*, meaning "man" or "warrior." The principal town in the Anderson Valley is Boonville, which is worthy of note because its founder was allegedly related to Daniel Boone and because—of particular interest to word lovers—it successfully developed its own unique dialect and perpetuated it for more than 100 years.

ANJOU • This wine region in the Loire Valley in France shares its etymology with that of its principal city, Angers. Both names came from the Latin *Andecavi*, which is what the Romans called the Gauls who were living there when the Romans arrived. History is written by the literate so we don't know what the Gauls themselves called the region. Nor do we we know the origin of *Andecavi*.

APERITIF • An aperitif is a drink taken before a meal on the theory that it "opens the appetite." From the Latin *aperire*, the word *aperitif* means "to open" and appeared in French as early as 1750, taking almost a century and a half to make it into English in 1894. Its first appearance in English was in the magazine *The Idler*, a publication notable for its contributors, including Arthur Conan Doyle, Mark Twain, and H. G. Wells.

APHID • In the 1860s, France—to its horror—encountered head-on the same mystery that had held back American winemaking since the Spanish began to establish vines in the 1500s and English settlers tried to follow suit at Jamestown in the early 1600s. Inexorably, French vineyards began dying, and it took decades to figure out the cause and implement a workable solution. The problem was—and still is—a tiny little aphid known as *phylloxera* (now going by the scientific name *Dactylasphaera vitifoliae*). Had those panicked vintners known, they would have appreciated the etymology of *aphid*.

10

Aphid is an anglicized version of *aphis*, the scientific Latin name given these little critters by Carl Linnaeus, the Swedish father of botanical and zoological taxonomy. The reason Linnaeus chose *aphis* for these bugs is uncertain, but the leading theory is that he did so based on the Greek word *apheides*. Aphids can multiply rapidly, so it is thought that Linnaeus chose this Greek root for its meaning of "unsparing." (See **phylloxera**, p. 134.)

APPELLATION CONTRÔLÉE • French for "controlled name" the full title is actually *appellation d'origine contrôlée*, meaning "controlled place name of origin." The French system evolved during the 1930s as a response to market challenges after phylloxera and mildew had damaged vineyards. The first published regulations in France came out in 1936 and have since been expanded and amended. They were first mentioned in English only in 1950, as their importance became clear to wine drinkers. The word *appellation* had already existed in English for almost 500 years and is closely related to our English word *appeal*. The Latin root meant not so much "name" as "to call," which makes the connection to *appeal* more understandable. The word *contrôlée* has an unexpected background. As you'd expect, it is a very similar word to our English *control*, but the Latin root actually broke into two words, *contra* and *rotulus*. Although the literal translation of this might be "against the roll," the figurative meaning was actually "duplicate register." In other words, you "control" something by checking details in a register. This is an etymological example of the Romans' practical project management techniques. Finally, the word *origin* also comes from Latin—from *oriri*, a very early root meaning "to arise" or "to be born." (See **Côte d'Or**, p. 61.)

ARGENTINA • Argentina produces more wine than any other South American nation and ranks fifth worldwide. This production amounts to a sizable slice of the Argentine economy. However, the region's first important exports were

11

precious metals, which gave rise to the country's name. In the 1500s, Spain established a presence in what is now Argentina and struck up a trading relationship with the natives already there. Among the commodities the natives had to offer were silver ornaments and jewelry. Thus, the region took on the name *Rio de la Plata*, meaning "river of silver." Spanish descended from Latin, and the Latin word for "silver" was *argentum*, so *Tierra Argentina*—the "Land of Silver"—was a naturally synonymous name.

AROMA • In the world of wine, aroma is sometimes seen as an early-stage attribute of the beverage-to-be. With luck, as the wine grows closer to drinking readiness, simpler aromas turn into a more complex bouquet. However, *aroma* has a longer pedigree in the world of food and drink than does *bouquet*. While *bouquet* only appeared as a word within the last 500 years—and only within the last 150 in relation to something you'd want to put in your mouth—the etymology of *aroma* runs back through English to the time of the Norman Conquest almost 1000 years ago. The word's meaning changed little as it moved from Greek through Latin to French and, finally, to English. In Middle English, *aroma* didn't mean only something you sensed with your nose; rather, it meant "spice," something to be experienced through eating, drinking, and smelling. Today, we distinguish herbs from spices—the former being plant foliage, and the latter being seeds, fruit, or bark. These distinctions were not so rigid in classical times. The Greek word *aroma* was more closely associated with herbs, while the Latin word referred more to spices.

ARROYO GRANDE VALLEY • The name of this small California winegrowing valley means "big stream" in Spanish. The Spanish word *arroyo* appeared in English in 1807 and evolved from a Medieval Latin word, *arrogium*, with the same meaning. *Arrogium* can be traced to the year 775. There does not seem to have been a forerunner word in Classical Latin however. Arroyo Seco is another wine area near Monterey tagged with the Spanish word for "stream." In this case, however, it is a dry stream; *seco*, which means "dry," comes from the Latin *siccus*.

ASTI • Wines such as Moscato d'Asti and, formerly, Asti Spumante (now simply Asti) take their name from the town of Asti in the northwest corner of Italy. The town of Asti in Roman times was called *Hasta* or *Asta* and for some time was known as *Hasta Pompeia*. This name was based on local lore that Pompey the Great had planted his spear there declaring the place the common property of Roman citizens; *hasta* means "spear" in Latin. Modern suggestion, however, is that the name is older and evolved from an Indo-European root *owis* meaning "sheep" and may have been a place for grazing.

AUCTION • Wine has been sold at auction for millennia, and the etymology of *auction* reflects this tradition since the word root was already use in Latin with this meaning. From *auctio*, meaning "increase," an auction works through a mechanism of increasing bids. The same root gave English the word *augment*.

AUSTRALIA • Australia is the world's seventh-largest producer of wine. If you look at an old map of the world, you are likely to see vast areas with little detail marked as *terra incognita*, meaning "unknown lands." As people went about exploring the world—and perhaps, more to the point, as they began documenting these explorations—the idea of an unknown southern land emerged. For centuries, this place was called *terra australis incognita*. You can extrapolate from the fact that *terra incognita* means "unknown lands" that *australis* means "southern." When the Dutch first mapped the coast of Australia, they called the place *New Holland*. The English were the first Europeans to permanently set up shop—with a penal colony at Port Jackson in New South Wales in 1788—but they continued to refer to the continent as *Terra*

Australis. In 1804, naval officer Matthew Flinders came up with the name *Australia*, which he thought "more agreeable to the ear." His boss Sir Joseph Banks didn't like this innovation, so Flinders didn't use it (as he'd hoped to) in the title of his report of his explorations in Terra Australis. He did, however, sneak it onto the map he included. The Admiralty finally picked up the neologism in 1824 when it issued updated charts of the continent.

AUSTRIA • Although Austria does not produce as much wine as Australia, it has been producing it for much longer. Its name also comes from a direction on the compass. Confusingly, though, while *Australia* means "south," *Austria* means "east." The difference is explained by the fact that while *Australia* evolved from a Latin word for "south," *Austria* came instead from a Germanic word meaning "east," the reference being to the area's easterly direction with respect to the empire of Charlemagne.

AUXERROIS • Several different types of grape are named Auxerrois but all take their names from the city of Auxerre in Burgundy. The city formerly also gave its name to the surrounding region. It warranted this importance due to its location on an old Roman road at the point where a bridge crosses the Yonne River. For most of human history having a bridge was a big deal for a town. The name of the town is said to be a combination of the Gaulish personal name *Autesio* and the Gaulish word *duron*, meaning "house" or "fort."

B

BACCHUS • The Greeks had their Dionysus—the god of wine—so the Romans had to have one too, and they called him *Bacchus*. That's the short version of the story. Since these are tales of mythology, the facts of the case are sometimes hard to pin down. On the one hand, there seems to have been a precursor to the Roman god of wine already abroad in what we now think of as Italy; he was *Liber*. On the other hand, the Greeks seemed to sometimes refer to Dionysus as *Bakchos* and some reports link this name to *bacca*, which is Latin for "berry." In any case, Bacchus has been adopted as the original party animal and has been captured in countless paintings and poems. Although there was no officially recognized festival of Bacchus in ancient Rome, this god did inspire enough of a following that the Roman senate banned celebrations in his name. Bacchanalia appears to have been a kind of sexual alcoholic cult that got out of hand. Bacchus was put to more constructive use within the past century, when he—with the help of German viticulturalist Peter Morio—encouraged a *ménage à trois* between the grape varieties Silvaner, Riesling, and Müller-Thurgau. The resulting new grape bears the Bacchus name and also bears admirable fruit in tough growing conditions.

BACO NOIR and BACO BLANC • These grape varieties are named in honor of François Baco, a French hybrid developer and teacher. Although the grapes are not seen as superstars in fine wine circles, the people who knew Baco thought enough of him to construct a substantial monument within a few years of his death. On either side of his stone bust are depicted scenes from the harvest that almost seem to be bowing down reverentially to Monsieur Baco.

BADEN • Like the English city of Bath, this large wine region in Germany is named for nearby hot springs that were used as baths. The etymology is Germanic. Although today we think of *bath* as having to do with washing, the root word denoted "heat" rather than "cleanliness."

BALANCE • While wine drinkers think of balance as a quality of the taste of wine—when the various elements of acidity, alcohol, fruit, sweetness, and tannins are in harmony—winegrowers think of balance as a quality also of the vine itself. They manage the growth of their crop by balancing leaf and fruit pruning to optimize quality grape production. This dual meaning of balance in the world of wine is fitting, given the etymology of the word *balance*. The Latin root *bilanx* literally broke down to mean "two plates," such as those you might see hanging on either side of a scale.

BALTHAZAR • A Balthazar is a wine bottle that holds the equivalent of 16 standard bottles of wine, which is to say 12 liters. The huge bottle is named after Balthazar or Belshazzar, the king of Babylon, who was also said to have been one of the three wise men. Mentioned in the biblical Book of Daniel, Balthazar is said to have "made a great feast to a thousand of his lords, and drank wine before the thousand." According to www.etymonline.com, the name in Babylonian is *Balat-shar-usur*, meaning "save the life of the king."

BANDOL • This red appellation from Provence is named after the port town from which these wines were once shipped worldwide. In the 11ᵗʰ century, the town was known as Bendoroi. The name's deeper meaning is uncertain, but the pre-Indo-European word *ben-d*, meaning "rock," has been suggested.

BAR • People drink wine in bars, and the reason bars are called *bars* is that there is usually a barrier blocking access to the source of the drinks. The entire establishment takes its name from the bar behind which the barkeep stands. This usage of *bar* first appeared in English when Shakespeare was in mid career. Although he wasn't the first to write about drinking at a bar, Shakespeare did use *bar* in that sense in *Twelfth Night*. The word arrived in English much earlier, back in the 12th century, referring to a stake of iron or wood. English got the word from French and French took it from Latin, although etymologists find a frustrating lack of evidence as to how the word got into Latin. It wasn't there in Classical Latin but seems to have arisen before Vulgar Latin became French. Once the word emerged, though, there seemed no stopping it. Most fat dictionaries list dozens of meanings for the word, not to mention related words. One of these that might relate to excessive time spent at a bar is the word *embarrass*. The contemporary understanding of "being embarrassed" might relate closely to "being ashamed." However, when the word first arose in English, it meant "to be blocked in achieving something." One of the things that blocked people was a lack of money, so for a while to be embarrassed meant "to be short of funds." It is this uncomfortable financial position that led to the word being nearly synonymous with *shame*.

BARBARESCO • Although it is a very civilized wine, the word *Barbaresco* means "barbarian" in Italian. It was not a marketing manager trying to emphasize rugged flavor or the strength of the wine who brought about this name. Instead, the wine takes its name from a village in northwest Italy. The village name dates from the era when the expanding Roman Empire pushed up against the Ligurians, who lived along the coast of the Mediterranean where the boot of Italy begins to merge with the rest of Europe. The Ligurians took refuge in and around the area of Barbaresco, and so the Romans called the woodlands *barbarica silva*, meaning "forest of the barbarians."

BARBAROSSA • This Italian name for a grape variety means "red beard" in Italian; the same grape variety is named *Barbaroux* in French. The reason is that the grape bunches have a reddish look to them. A few historical figures have shared the name Barbarossa based on having red beards; they include Frederic I, King of Germany and Holy Roman Emperor in the mid 1100s, and a powerful Turkish sea captain.

BARBERA • Barbera is one of the most widely planted vines in Italy, but this name for it didn't appear much before 200 years ago. It is suspected, however, that the grape was a stalwart in northwest Italy for centuries before that. Although the word *barbera* means "wife of a barber" and was also a slang term for "prostitute," these meanings are probably coincidental. The true etymology of the name is likely similar to that of the town of Barbaresco—that is, the name was derived from the region's status as a barbarian holdout against the Roman Empire. (See **Barbaresco**, p. 17.)

BARDOLINO • These wines take their name from a town and region on the eastern shores of Lake Garda, Italy's largest lake, on the flatter lands south of the Alps. The town is said to have been named when Germanic speakers invaded the area from the north after the fall of the Roman Empire; the name may have been a personal name from that period. An alternative etymology is that the area was named after a daughter of a local king.

BAROLO • A bold and famous wine, Barolo takes its name from a village in northwestern Italy that was first recorded 800 years ago as *Villa Barogly* and later as *Barrolo* and *Barollo*. The most likely origin of the town's name may be the Celtic term *bas reul*, meaning "low place," since the village is in a valley, while many surrounding towns sit perched on hilltops. In 1875, British publisher, journalist, and wine writer Henry Vizetelly became the first person to use the word in reference to wine in an English document. Vizetelly learned about wine while working as a correspondent in Paris.

BAROSSA VALLEY • This Australian wine region's name slipped down off the hills to the east. In 1837, surveyor William Light found his way into this region and named these ranges *Barossa* after a battle in Spain in which he had fought for the British. The Battle of Barossa was of little consequence to France or Spain, who were the main combatants. It was important to Light, though, because his service there resulted in his promotion from lieutenant to colonel. During the battle, the British were forced to defend and retake a hillside by the name of *Vigia de la Barrosa*, while some of their allies fled. The Spanish word *barrosa* means "muddy."

BARREL • Sometime in the centuries after the beginning of the Common Era (once called the Christian Era), people who sold wine throughout the Mediterranean stopped using amphorae as shipping and storage containers, and began using animal skins and wooden barrels. The change was likely driven by economic factors, barrels and skins being easier to produce and lighter to transport, but no one knows for sure. The switch has frustrated modern historians, since barrels and skin sacks tend to turn into dust over the centuries, while an amphora lasts for millennia and can help researchers decode ancient trade patterns among the buyers and sellers of wine and other goods. No one is sure why a barrel is called a *barrel*, but the word entered English from French. Pretty well all of the languages that descended from Latin have a similar word, yet, mysteriously, Classical Latin didn't seem to have an ancestor word.

BARSAC • The Bordeaux sweet wine called *Barsac* takes its name from a place name first seen in the 13th century that is derived from *Barcios*, a Gaulish personal name.

BASILICATA • This Italian region has retained its name from the time of the Byzantine Empire, which the Greeks called *Basileia ton Rhomaion.* The empire or kingdom was so named based on the Greek word *basileus,* meaning "king." This word root shows up in such unlikely places as J. K. Rowling's *Harry Potter* books, where the giant snake called a *basilisk* is borrowed from classical mythology and takes its name from a crown-like growth on its head.

BEAUJOLAIS • Famously, many wines from Beaujolais in France are supposed to be enjoyed young, and the *nouveau* or "new" of Beaujolais Nouveau has inspired plenty of other nouveau wines. If youth and beauty are related, perhaps it is etymologically appropriate that nouveau wines come from Beaujolais, since *beau* means "beautiful." The region is named after the town of Beaujeu, which might be mistranslated as "beautiful game." The *-jeu* suffix is actually believed to have evolved from the Latin *jugum,* meaning "hill," hence *Beaujolais* becomes "from the beautiful hills."

BEAUNE • The important area of Burgundy known as the Côte de Beaune takes its name from the city of Beaune, which traces its history to its founding as a military camp by Julius Caesar in 52 BCE. The most likely origin of the name *Beaune* is the Latin *Belena Castro,* meaning "fortress of Belenos." Belenos was a Gaulish-Celtic god who has been likened to Apollo.

BEER • The etymology of the word *beer* remains in dispute. According to one theory, *beer* is related to some of the oldest words for "drink." In Indo-European, the word for "drink" may have been *poi.* Over the ages, this may have mutated to *bibo* and formed the basis not only for *beer* but also for the Latin *imbibere,* literally "in drink," which is an ancestor of our words *imbibe* ("to drink") and *beverage* ("a drink"). If this theory is true, the word likely passed through Latin into Germanic and, thus, into Old English. That doesn't mean the drink beer itself followed this route, since it appears that beer was widely known and consumed across Europe and beyond, and that it was made as early as 8000 years ago. An alternative theory for the etymology of the word *beer* is that a Germanic root word evolved from the same source as that for *barley*. This is a plausible theory based both on the way beer is made and on the fact that the Romans who spread their Latin so broadly were much more enthusiastic drinkers of wine than of beer.

BEFUDDLE • The word *fuddle*, meaning "drink," appeared in English in 1588. *Befuddle* didn't appear until 1887. Although we might think it is synonymous with the word *confuse*, *befuddle* took its original meaning from *fuddle* and is defined in part by *The Oxford English Dictionary* as "to make stupid with tippling."

BERRY • When the word *berry* was first used in English, it applied exclusively to grapes. *Berry* was one of the words that crossed the English Channel with the Anglo-Saxons to become one of the original words in Old English. Most Germanic languages have a relative to our word *berry*, but other Indo-European languages don't use the word. One source suggests that the word *berry* may trace back to the Indo-European root *bha*, meaning "to shine," based on the fact that it is a brightly colored fruit, though this seems somewhat speculative. Another theory is that the Germanic root is related to the Old English word *basu*, meaning "red." As an Old English word, *berry* showed up in writings more than 1000 years ago, the first that we know of being by a Benedictine abbot named Aelfric. Aelfric mentions berries being eaten out of a vineyard, so the reference to grapes is clear and unambiguous. Aelfric is an important person in the world of English etymology because he was a prolific writer in English when few other people in England were writing at all, and most of those who were, were writing in Latin. The reason Aelfric wrote in English is interesting, too. Because most of what was considered important learning in his time was recorded in Latin, most English people were not only unable to read it, but they were also unable to understand it being read to them. Aelfric was worried about their eternal souls and felt that the religious understandings circulating in folklore were inaccurate. He wanted to correct those misunderstandings, and he felt that he was up against a deadline. Aelfric was writing in the late 900s and he, among many others, believed that with the year 1000 would come the Day of Judgment.

BINGE • People sometimes go on eating binges, but this word arose to describe binge drinking. Barrels were formerly used to contain wine or any number of other goods. One of the steps in the manufacture of barrels was to soak the completed barrel in water so that the wooden staves would swell. As they plumped up with absorbed water, they pushed harder against their neighboring barrel staves and closed up any little cracks that might have existed that would have allowed the barrel to leak. This soaking process was called "putting the barrel to binge." Hence, to *binge* meant "to soak." It only makes sense that when drinkers were out soaking up vast quantities of wine or beer, they too were said to be *binging*. The word first appeared in print with this meaning in 1854; it wasn't applied to eating until 1937.

BLANC • This French word for "white" can apply to white wine or, in the case of *blanc de blancs*, be used to mean "white wine from white grapes." *Blanc* is the French version of the Italian word *bianco* and the Spanish word *blanco*. All of these words popped up in the language that had once been Latin but was not yet quite French, Italian, or Spanish and is sometimes known as Romanic. The root from which they sprang is thought to be a Germanic word along the lines of *blancoz*. Some sources point to an Indo-European root meaning "shine." Now try to think of an English word that might have evolved from the same source. Are you drawing a blank? If so, you've hit on it; it's *blank*. Despite its Germanic roots, no Old English relative has been firmly established, and it took the French of the Norman Conquest of 1066 to bring *blanc* and thence *blank* into English. It had made the transition by the early 1300s but retained its "white" meaning until at least the late 1500s, not truly taking on our "empty" or "not written on" meaning until well into the 1800s.

BLIND • In most cases, a "blind tasting" does not involve tasters wearing blindfolds. Instead, it involves tasters sampling wines without having seen the bottles from which they were poured. According to *The Oxford Companion to Wine* blindfolding tasters can even cause misidentification between red and white varieties. That is appropriate to the etymology of the word *blind*, which has Old English and Germanic roots and is thought to have come from the Indo-European word *bhlendhos*, which meant "confusion" or "obscurity" rather than "lack of vision."

BLOOM • With respect to wine, the word *bloom* applies not only to the subtle flowers that will later become grapes; the dusty-looking outer layer of those grapes is also called the *bloom*. The word root goes back to the Indo-European *bhel* or *bhlo*. This word evolved through Germanic languages into Old Norse before it entered Middle English as *bloom*, meaning "flower," circa 1200. In the early 1600s, the word was applied to the powdery layer on fruit. The related word *blossom* grew up in parallel within Old English. Both words were partially displaced after the same Indo-European root, having become *flos* in Latin, arrived from French and gave us *flower*.

BLUSH • People have been blushing for a very long time. It's one of those things we have all experienced. Words that describe broadly common experiences are often words that resist changes to meaning and pronunciation. So it makes sense that the word *blush* hasn't changed much over centuries. Even though the word can't be documented before 1325, the ancestors of *blush* existed in Old English, and a few similar words appeared in Old Norse and some other Germanic languages. Some sources suggest a connection to words meaning "torch," as might be appropriate for something that glows red. Others link *blush* to the same Indo-European root meaning "shine" that may have contributed to the French word *blanc*, meaning "white." Blush wine is not white wine, but often it isn't quite rosé, either. The first citation in which *blush* is applied to wine comes from a 1979 *Washington Post* report on a California wine promotional tasting. The journalist laments the sparse attendance for these underrated wines, one of which was a Mill Creek Vineyards Cabernet Blush 1978 from Sonoma. During the 1980s, the popularity of blush wine began to accelerate, and some wineries were surprised to discover that Mill Creek Vineyards had trademarked the word *blush* and that anyone trying to sell wine labeled as *blush* was obliged to pay royalties to the trademark owners.

BODY • People have long struggled to come up with language that could adequately describe the tastes and aromas of wine. It's safe to say that a universally understood vocabulary has yet to emerge. To say a wine is *full bodied* is one of the more successful expressions of the wine experience, communicating a feeling of fullness and roundness in the mouth. But even this expression is only a partial success; if you're thinking, "What does 'roundness in the mouth' mean?" then I've made my point. The word *body* is an unusual one in that it has been an English word for as long as there has been English (the first citation occurred circa 890) but appears to have no etymology outside of English at all. There was one wispy trace back in Old High German, the possible relation *potah*, but for a word that is so ubiquitous in English, it is strange that *body* has no siblings in other Indo-European tongues.

BORACHIO • In William Shakespeare's play *Much Ado About Nothing*, Borachio is a secondary character who at one point, while tipsy, divulges some information critical to the plot. Perhaps not coincidentally, during Shakespeare's lifetime the word *borachio* meant "a leather wine bag" and, by extension, "a drunkard"; the word was borrowed from Spanish or Italian.

BORDEAUX • Bordeaux wine takes its name from the region in southwest France of the same name, which in turn takes its name from the port city there. The city of Bordeaux was known from Roman times as both a trading port and a source of wine. The modern name evolved from the Latin of the Romans, who knew the place as *Burdigala*. It is thought that this name came from two words, *burd* and *gala*, that may have originated in the language of the people of Aquitaine. This is a fairly loose definition, since Aquitaine covered a large area of what is now southwest France that was populated by people who did not see themselves as a single large group. This fact is made more evident by another Roman name for the area, *Novempopulania*, meaning "country of nine peoples." *The Oxford English Dictionary* cites the word *Bordeaux* as having entered English in the late 1500s. Based on several *OED* citations, we may deduce that the word's arrival was celebrated with some overindulgence. For example, a 1570 Scottish poem includes a "stomack owersett with Burdeous"; in 1576, a hangover was described as a "Burdeaux hammer beating in [one's] head"; and in 1597, Shakespeare had Falstaff accused of consuming "a whole Marchants Venture of Burdeux-Stuffe"—that is, an entire ship's hold full.

BORRADO DAS MOSCAS • This is a Portuguese grape variety known as *Bical* outside the Dao region. *Borrado das Moscas* means "fly droppings" and is thought to have been given to the grape because of a speckled pattern on the skin.

BOTTLE • When people first began speaking of *bottles* in English, the bottles to which they referred were not made of glass. In 1375, the word made its official transition from the French of William the Conqueror to the English of John Wycliffe. Those bottles would have been leather and the French word would have evolved from *butticula*, a Latin word meaning "small cask." This root makes *bottle* etymologically related to the synonym for *cask*, *butt*. Glass bottles as we know them did not become widely available until the 1600s and, even then, they were manufactured according to the skill of the maker rather than to any standard size or shape. People continued to buy their wine in casks to protect themselves from being shortchanged as a consequence of the unknown bottle volumes. Once purchased, the wine would be transferred into bottles owned by the buyer and reused again and again. John Wycliffe's name comes up regularly in English etymology, because Wycliffe was particularly keen on translating Latin documents into the language of the common people. Many English words, therefore, made their first appearance on paper from his pen. We can assume that *bottle* was already being used in spoken English or Wycliffe would not have chosen it in translation. The Roman Catholic Church did not look favorably on Wycliffe's translations at the time. Even after he was dead and gone, the church carried a grudge so strong that eventually his bones were dug up and burned, and the ashes thrown into the River Swift. (See **aging**, p. 4.)

BOUQUET • The bouquet of wine is its smell. Some distinguish *bouquet* from *aroma* by likening the complex mixture of smells in a mature wine's bouquet to the mixture of buds in a bouquet of flowers. For these people, the aroma is a less sophisticated smell of the fruit itself. The word *bouquet* came into English from French in the early 1700s but wasn't applied to wines until the 1800s. In French in the 1500s and later in English, *bouquet* first applied to collections of flowers before being extended as a metaphor to wine. The word root behind *bouquet* is believed to be of Germanic origin with a meaning of "wood"; the ending of *bouquet* is a diminutive, so the word literally means "little wood." The idea is that a *bouquet* is a "little wood" akin to a small bush covered in flowers. Our modern floral bouquets include a collection of stems that mimic such a bush. It is a happy coincidence that "wood" lies at the root of *bouquet*, since aging in contact with wood often adds to a wine's complexity.

BOURGEAIS • Also Côtes de Bourg, this area in Bordeaux is named for a village that takes its name in turn from the Germanic root that gave *burg* the meaning of "town." It was known as early as 1169 as *de Bergo*. (See **bourgeois** and **Bourgueil**, below.)

BOURGEOIS • In the French system of wine classification, *cru bourgeois* represents those wines and wineries that fall below the more aristocratic classifications. If the best wines are to be consumed with gourmet food, then perhaps bourgeois wines should be quaffed with hamburgers. Such a food pairing is etymologically appropriate, since *bourgeois* evolved from the Latin root *bergus*, meaning "town," and hamburgers are named for the city of Hamburg, which gets its name partly from the same root. The Romans had earlier adopted *bergus* from the Germanic. The boroughs of New York and the city of Edinburgh were also named from the same root. The earliest version was likely the Germanic *burg* and meant "to protect." The word was applied to castles and fortified towns before being applied to towns in general. Thus the application of *bourgeois* to wines is a designation of middle-class status analogous to *townspeople*, who are beneath *nobility* but above the *peasants*.

BOURGUEIL • This area in the Loire Valley in France is named for a village that in turn takes its name from the same Germanic root that produced *bourgeois*, above (and

Pittsburgh, for that matter). The village was known as early as 990 as *Burgolium*.

BRANDY • While at a dinner party in 1779, the dictionary maker Samuel Johnson proclaimed that claret was the drink of boys and port the drink of men, but to be a hero, one must drink brandy. He explained that brandy had the strongest taste and also brought soonest whatever benefits alcoholic drinks can bring. The word *brandy* is an abbreviation of *brandy-wine*, which came to English in 1622 from the Dutch word *brandewijn*. This Dutch source literally means "burned wine," but the name doesn't relate to whatever strong taste Dr. Johnson appreciated. Instead, it relates to the fact that brandy was one of the first distilled liquors to become popular in Europe. The fact that the source was a Dutch word underlines the leading role that traders from the Netherlands played in popularizing brandy. The "burned" attribute of this drink comes from the distillation process and, particularly, its early technology. Distillation had been known for some centuries, learned from the Arab world, but it had been severely restricted by law until the 1500s in Europe. The Dutch found an unexploited source of wine along the west coast of France in the region of Charente and set themselves up as resellers to the rest of Europe. They found that distilling this wine made shipping easier in two ways. Not only did distillation prevent wine from becoming vinegar while in transit; it also took up less room on the ships. Today, distillation takes place in huge stills, but back when the Dutch product was named, the technology was more rudimentary. In its earliest implementations, a pot of wine was set to boil on a fire, thus "burned." The alcohol was captured when it evaporated before the water portion of the wine came to a boil. Wool mats covered the pots and the alcohol condensed back into a liquid as it moved through the wool.

BREATHING • In the comic strip *Hagar the Horrible*, the lead character, a Viking, is seen pulling a cork from a bottle and allowing it to breathe. He quickly grows concerned that the wine isn't breathing and so resorts to mouth-to-mouth resuscitation, upending the bottle against his thirsty lips. Although wine does change its character upon exposure to air and oxygen, since the area exposed to air in the neck of a bottle is relatively tiny, allowing a bottle to "breathe" before serving it has far less effect than the pouring the wine out or swirling it in the glass. The idea that a wine might breathe suggests that it takes in oxygen as we do when we breathe, but the word *breathe* has not always meant "take in" air. It once exclusively meant "expel" and, in fact, the expelling of something other than air. The ultimate root of *breathe* and *breath* is the Indo-European *bhretos*, which is thought to have referred to steam and cooking odors coming off a meal on the fire. The parent word worked its way through Germanic and into Old English and, even there, at first referred to odor and smells given off. It was almost the time of Chaucer in the 14th century before the word took on the sense of "in and out" that we give it today.

BRETON • In the French region of Loire, the grape Cabernet Franc is often called *Breton*. Most sources suggest this name originated in 1631, when Cardinal Richelieu assigned the task of a major planting to one Abbot Breton, the name of the manager of the operation thus becoming affixed to the newly planted vine variety. Abbot Breton would in turn have gotten his name from an ancestral connection to Brittany, that most northwestern part of modern France. However, the French writer Rabelais refers in 1534 to Breton wine. That clearly predates Abbot Breton's involvement and so throws the 1631 origin into question. It doesn't make it impossible, though, since Rabelais may have been referring not to the grape name but instead to the same region that gave the Abbot his name.

BROKER • A broker is a trader who acts as a middleman. The word shows up in English documents starting in the 1300s from French. One theory on the word's etymology is that, during the time when Latin was morphing into French, the word *brocco* or *brocca* meant "spike" or "piercing instrument." Such tools may have been used to open casks of wine in order to sell the contents, thus giving the sellers their title of *broker*. Not all etymologists agree with this theory. An alternative etymology is that the word *broker* is related to the Spanish word *alboroque*, which means "sealing the deal."

BROUILLY • This area of Beaujolais in France has been known for its vineyards since Roman times. The Roman name was *Brulliacus* but its meaning is unknown.

BUGEY • The name of this winegrowing region in eastern France is a contraction of its former Latin name, *pagus Bellicenis*, which means "district of Belicius." That name was based on its then-capital city, Belley.

BUNCH • Grapes grow in bunches, but the word *bunch* is a bit of a mystery to etymologists. It appeared in English in the early 1300s from unknown sources, then changed its meaning. The earliest example of the word gives it a meaning similar to "bump," as opposed to our understanding of "a group" or "collection." In 1398, a camel is described as having two bunches on his back. Within a century, *bunch* began to mean "a collection"—at first, a collection of straw. Although some theorize that the word evolved as an imitation of the sound of something going "bump," others suggest a link to the Flemish word *bondje*, meaning "small bundle."

BURGUNDY • *Burgundy* is both the name of a region of France and of the wine that comes from that region. The place is named after a Germanic tribe known as the Bergundii who settled there in the 5th century. It was in the same century that the Anglo-Saxons settled Britain and similarly gave England its name, based on their tribal name, the *Angles*. The Bergundii are reported in Roman documents, and there are two schools of thought as to the origin of *Burgundia* as a Latin word. One possibility might be that it was based on the Gothic word *baurgjans*, meaning "fort dwellers." The second theory is that the name means "highlanders." In either case, the name's origin traces back to the Indo-European root *bhrghu*, meaning "elevated," which contributed to the Germanic root *burg* or *berg*, meaning "fort" and later "town." (See **bourgeois**, p. 27.)

BUTLER • To those of us who don't have a squad of domestic servants busily working around the house, the hierarchy of household staff may be a bit of a mystery. A butler is the head of the household as far as the hired help goes and is the most trusted of all the domestic servants. This respect is reflected in the very word *butler*. The butler has always been trusted with the most valuable assets of a house, including the keys to the wine cellar. *Butler* comes from French and means "bottle bearer." The first citation in English is circa 1250.

BUTT • A butt was a cask or barrel, and the word appeared in English in the 1400s. Older related words had been around since Old English and *bottle*, also a related word, preceded *butt* into English from French by about a century. These days, we don't often encounter the word *butt* referring to a "barrel," yet it still remains in everyday use when we gossip, because it's folded within the word *scuttlebutt*. Thirsty sailors used to gather around a barrel of water aboard ship. The barrel was called the *scuttle butt* because, just as a ship might be scuttled (meaning "intentionally sunk") by cutting a hole in her hull, a hole had been cut in the side of the barrel to permit access the drinking water. Just as we refer to *water-cooler conversation* today, the sailors often exchanged their gossip at the scuttle butt, and thus the word *scuttlebutt* was born.

C

CABERNET • *Cabernet* sometimes appears as a word on its own, but when it does, it is usually being used as an abbreviation of *Cabernet Sauvignon* or perhaps *Cabernet Franc*. The first appearance of *Cabernet* in English was in 1833 in a book by Cyrus Redding entitled *A History and Description of Modern Wines*. However, it didn't actually appear as *Cabernet*; instead, it appeared as *carbenet*. In other places, it has appeared as *carbonet*. All sources point to French as the source of *Cabernet*. Although French dictionaries identify *Cabernet*'s etymology as unknown, with French's Latin roots, plus the dark color of Cabernet Sauvignon and Cabernet Franc grapes, it's easy to conceive that the name could have evolved from *carbon*, a Latin word meaning "charcoal." A word ending with "t" sometimes denotes a diminutive and so could suggest *Cabernet* means "little coal." The earliest French citation for *cabrunet*, in 1761, predates the English citation for *carbenet*. French sources agree that, while evidence is inconclusive, the Latin *carbon* is likely the best starting point for this etymology.

CADILLAC • For most people, the name *Cadillac* is more likely to evoke a prestigious brand of car than a wine grown in the Cadillac area of Bordeaux. Yet the names have the same source and similarly rich stories. The fortified town of Cadillac was purpose built in the 13th century for a nobleman who needed river access for a recently acquired castle. The name appeared in the written record as *Cadilacum* in 1306 and according to the *Dictionnaire étymologique des noms de lieux en France* comes from the Gallo-Roman family name *Cadeilhan*. Some histories portray the castle owning nobleman as a representative of the English government that then controlled the area. His name, however, was Jean I de Grailly which hints at the fact that the English government was itself French at the time. The second story also has to do with the founding of a town. Approximately 400 years after the founding of Cadillac, a fellow named Antoine Laumet was born about 100 miles away. He emigrated and became what Canadian author Agnes Laut called one of the "great early heroes in North American history." Historian William John Eccles expressed it a little differently, calling Laumet "one of the worst scoundrels ever to set foot in New France." Laut admired Laumet because his founding of Detroit was only one small item on his list of accomplishments. The reason Eccles disagrees is that Laumet lied, cheated, and invented noble titles, personal histories, and family crests to enhance his power and stature. The reason the car is called a *Cadillac* is that Antoine Laumet gave himself the title *de La Mothe, sieur de Cadillac*, as if he were a nobleman owning property in the French town.

CALABRIA • This southern Italian region is named after its early occupants, whose own name is thought to have evolved from a pre-Indo-European word *kalabra* or *galabra* meaning "rock."

CALIFORNIA • Hugh Johnson and Jancis Robinson's *World Atlas of Wine* states that "California is as important to the world of wine as wine is important to California." There have been whole books written about how California got its name. The facts are these: In 1510, a Spanish writer named Garci Ordonez de Montalvo produced a novel called *Las sergas de Esplandian.* Therein he related the tale of the island of California, where beautiful women were ruled by their queen, Calafia. Within a few decades, the Spanish were exploring the west coast of North America, and it is likely that sometime during this period they began naming some of the places along the coast after this mythical place. At first, it was not clear that the huge peninsula now known as Baja California was in fact a peninsula; some explorers thought it was an island. The name *California* took a while to stick to maps. For some time, it shifted up and down the coast, among claims and counter-claims by European powers as to what lands belonged to whom.

CAMPANIA • The name of this southwestern Italian region comes from the same Latin source that is thought to have given Champagne its name. *Campus* meant a field, plain, or open space.

CANADA • Not a major wine world power, Canada nevertheless holds its own in icewine, the sweet dessert wine produced from grapes that have frozen on the vine. In 1536, Jacques Cartier was trying to establish a beachhead for France in the new world. As he explored the St. Lawrence River, he kept meeting the locals who spoke an Iroquois language. They regularly referred to the places they were going to, or the places they had come from, as *kanata*. What they were actually saying was "village," but Jacques Cartier didn't know that and assumed the entire landmass was called *kanata*.

CANARY • Canary wines put in several appearances in the plays of William Shakespeare and continued to gain popularity for the century following his lifetime. These wines were not called *canary* because of a yellow color but because they came from the Canary Islands off the coast of Africa. The birds we know as *canaries* are named because their ancestors were captured on those same islands. It was the Romans who named the islands, calling them the Isles of Dogs, which since the Latin word for dog is *canus*, came out as *Canaria insula*.

CANTEEN • A thirsty cowboy in an old western movie might take a swig from his canteen, but a soldier might go buy a little something at the base canteen. The reason that this word applies both to drinking containers and military retail outlets is that, back in Italian, *cantina* meant "wine cellar" as well as "wine seller." The word adhered to the retail operation, based on the location of the supplies. French then took the word *cantine* out of the cellar and applied it to a case for holding bottles, from which English acquired the word referring to a drinking container. Both senses tumbled simultaneously into the English written record in 1744 in the same book, entitled *The life and adventures of Matthew Bishop of Deddington in Oxfordshire.* The initial Italian meaning of a "wine cellar" arose from the Latin word root *cant*, which had evolved from *canto* to refer to something "sectioned off"—as one would do to a wine cellar. However, *cant* originally meant "edge," because *cantus* was the name for the iron rim around a wagon wheel.

CAPSULE • Over the top of the cork on a wine bottle is the capsule or foil. The term *capsule* was first used for this covering in 1858 in English but not until 1864 in French. In other applications, the word had already been around for a few centuries in both languages, since it arose from the Latin word *capsula*, meaning "little box." *Foil* is more self-explanatory as a name since many bottles, particularly of sparkling wine, are topped with a crimped layer of laminated metal foil. Most people have aluminum foil in their kitchen, so the concept of *foil* as "a thin sheet of metal" is well understood. Yet these thin layers of metal are called *foil* by analogy. They are named because they are thin like the leaf of a tree, and the Latin word for a leaf was *folium*, closely related to our word *foliage*.

CARAFE • The word we use to describe this container from which wine is sometimes served came into English from French and is first cited in 1786. The root word was the Arabic *gharafa*, meaning "to dip up water," and it had moved through Italian before getting to French. As such, it is one of the relatively few English words that do not originate from an Indo-European language family. Arabic and Hebrew, among others, grew out of the Semitic family of languages.

CARBON DIOXIDE • The bubbles in Champagne are the merest lingering hint of the much larger volumes of carbon dioxide that are produced as must ferments into wine. The word *carbon*, of course, refers to an element. It was not named until the 1780s, when it was recognized as the main constituent in such things as coal and charcoal, for which the Latin name was *carbo*. Some sources suggest that the Latin word came from an earlier root word *kar*, meaning "fire." (See **oxidation**, pp. 130.)

CARDINAL • Cardinal is a grape variety usually grown for eating as opposed to winemaking and named for its red color. It is the most popular table grape in the world, so you've likely eaten it. It was created in Fresno, California, in 1939, when E. Snyder and F. Harmon crossed two existing varieties of grape, Flame Tokay and Ribier—or at least thought they had. DNA testing has since shown that Flame Tokay wasn't at the party that night, though it hasn't shown just who was there instead. A type of bird is also known as a *cardinal* based on its red color, and the association between the color and the word *cardinal* goes back to the Roman Catholic Church. Red is the traditional color worn by cardinals of the church, but these religious figures are called *cardinals* because of the etymology of the word *cardinal*. In Latin, *cardinem* means "hinge" and *cardinalis* "pertaining to a hinge." The work that cardinals do within the church is supposed to be so critical that they take their titles because things "turn" on their role.

CARIGNANE • In France this grape is called *Carignan* but it's named for its Spanish origin where it's known as *Cariñena* after a town in the north east of the country. The Spanish town has had its name since the time of the Romans and was mentioned by Pliny the Elder as *Carinius*. It was probably named based on the Roman personal name of a landowner. There is also a village called *Carignan* just east of the city of Bordeaux and some people have attributed the grape's name to this French source, arguing that the Spanish region doesn't produce as much wine or grow very much of this sort of grape. Yet based on the patterns of use of the grape name over time and through various languages, the Spanish source is considered most likely.

CARMEL VALLEY • This California wine region takes its name from the early Spanish explorers. In 1603, Sebastián Vizcaíno commanded a ship traveling north along the west coast of North America. Onboard were three friars of the Carmelite order, also known as the White Friars. When Vizcaíno espied the river now known as the Carmel River, he named it, it is believed, to honor these three and their holy mission. The name itself is much older, the religious order having taken its name from Mount Carmel, near the ancient city of Haifa in Israel. However, this name is remarkably suitable for a winegrowing region, because its ancient Hebrew meaning is "garden," "orchard," or "vineyard," suggesting that wine was grown on Mount Carmel long ago.

CARMENÈRE and CARMENET • These two names of grape varieties may be related in their etymology, although that is far from clear. The *Dictionnaire des noms de cépages de France* speculates that the name *Carmenère* may be based on a root word *Carmen*—referring to another type of grape, said to be a small-berried variety from Medoc—plus a suffix related to *noire* or "black." Without other evidence to go on, *Carmenet* is considered in the same light. Both are seen as suspiciously similar—as words—to *Cabernet*. It has also been suggested that *Carmenère* may stem from the same Latin root as the English words *carmine* and *crimson*; both words describing shades of red. If this is the case, the etymology gets more interesting because this Latin root had earlier been adopted from an Arabic word *qirmiz* that referred to a kind of red bug used to produce red dye. These insects live on oak trees and for a time were mistaken for a sort of red berry and even used in medicines. (See **Cabernet**, p. 33.)

CARNEROS • This is an area at the junction of the Napa and Sonoma valleys in California; *Los Carneros* means "the sheep" in Spanish. We might assume that this land was used for grazing before the land grants that named it were written.

CAROUSE • The word *carouse* first appeared in English in 1567, when William Shakespeare was just three years old. Words continue to change meaning, and *carouse* may today be assuming some of the meaning of the word *cruise*, since it seems to have acquired a sense of motion. Historically, though, *carouse* has always meant "to drink." It is a contraction of a German phrase, *gar-aus trinken*, which means "all-out drinking." In this case, "all-out drinking" doesn't mean putting a full "all-out" effort into your consumption; instead, the sense is "quickly drain the glass."

CASE • When buying wine in bulk, if you are not buying a container ship full—and most of us aren't—you are likely buying by the case. A case conventionally holds 12 bottles. The word *case* appeared in English around the year 1300 in a poem that purported to be a history of the world to that point. The poem is called *Cursor Mundi*, which means "runner of the world." The title is Latin but the poetry is in Middle English. Like many Middle English words, *case* had recently been adopted into English from French (if you can call adoption within a few centuries "recent"). The French word had come from the Latin root *capere*, which means "to take" or "hold." *The Oxford English Dictionary* dates the first use of *case* for a container for wine bottles to 1745.

CASK • In the mid 1500s, the word *cask* came into English, apparently from French. It refers to a wooden barrel, but the word root may more specifically refer to the flat ends of the barrel. For some reason, that root seems to mean "broken potshards." There must be an interesting story behind that, but the best etymological minds have yet to uncover it. Wine barrels and casks are sometimes plagued by insects called *bore-bugs* that find the wine-soaked wood particularly delicious. Needless to say, having them drill little holes into the cask is not helpful to its ability to contain the wine. Some cellarmasters apply a strip of willow or hickory wood around the outside of the ends of the barrel, in hopes that the bugs will find these hoops equally delicious and less difficult to chew than the oak of the barrel itself. Holes left by bore-bugs range from the size of a pencil lead down to needle width. Such holes are repaired with a special plug called a *spile* that is etymologically related to the word *splinter.*

CASSIS • This word has several wine connections. *Cassis* is French for "blackcurrant," and people sometimes describe the flavor or bouquet of a wine as having hints of cassis or blackcurrant. Cassis is also a tiny winegrowing region near Marseille on the Mediterranean in France. Finally, cassis is a sweet fruit syrup made from blackcurrants that can be added to white wines that seem too dry to be enjoyed as is. With respect to the berry, the Latin root of *cassis* derives from the impression of spices in the flavor of blackcurrant. The Latin *casia* and Greek *kassia* refer to a kind of alternative cinnamon, a spice made from dried bark. The name of this spice has been also connected to the Hebrew *qasiah*, which is said to derive from a word meaning "to strip off," as one would do to the bark. Some sources even extend the etymology into the Far East, suspecting the word came to the Middle East and Europe with the spice trade. *Blackcurrant* too is of some etymological interest. These berries are not genetically related to grapes, but currants are. The word *currant* was once *Corinth*, after the Greek city, and came into English in the 1300s from the French *raisins de Corinthe.* It was the late 1500s before *currant* was used as part of the name of redcurrants and blackcurrants. The French region of Cassis has a different etymology. The region takes its name from a town that in the 2nd century was known as *Tutelae Charsitanae*, of which *Cassis* is a contraction. The first part of its old name derives from the Latin *tutela*, meaning "keeper" or "guardian." The second part is thought to suggest an ancient word *kar*, meaning rock or stone.

CASTELLI ROMANI • *Castelli Romani* is Italian for "Castles of Rome." This wine region southeast of Rome was named for the castles built to house the aristocrats who have summered there since classical times. The name of the city of *Rome*, according to legend, comes from the personal name of *Romulus*, one of the twins supposedly raised by wolves to later found the city. This traditional but unlikely source competes with an unproven theory that the city took its name instead from the Tiber River, at a time when the river was called *Roma* or *Ruma*. That name may have been of Etruscan origin or related to the Greek *rhien*, meaning "to flow." (See **château**, p. 45.)

CELLAR • When a baseball team is described as being *in the cellar*, there is no ambiguity as to which floor the cellar might be on; it's in the basement, at the bottom. Storing wine in the cellar is recommended on the theory that, below ground level, temperature swings are less extreme and it's generally darker; both are good things when it comes to storing wine. But although the etymology of *cellar* does point to careful storage, it does not derive from any "below ground" meaning. At first in French, and then when it arrived in English in the 13th century, *cellar* referred to a storeroom, storehouse, or pantry. At that time, there was no sense of relative altitude wrapped into the word; the cellar could have been upstairs. Before becoming French, the Latin *cellarium* also meant storeroom; the ultimate root of the Latin word is thought to be the Indo-European word *kel*, which meant to "cover," "conceal," or "save." The assumption that such storerooms were below ground level invaded the word's meaning slowly, so it's impossible to say exactly when our current meaning became predominant.

CÉPAGE • Most French wines are sold according to their region or vineyard of growth and not by grape type. Those that are sold by grape type are sold according to their cépage, since *cépage* is the French word for vine variety. Though in other places, selling wines according to grape type is very popular—and of some advantage to producers, since they can more easily segment product lines—in France *vins de cépage* have been looked upon with some disrespect. The word *cépage* first appeared in French in 1573 and hasn't made it into many English dictionaries yet. *Cépage* means "of the cep," and *cep* is a French word that came from the Latin *cippus*, meaning "stake," such as a stick used to tie up vines. However, *cep* also has a sense of "stock," that first woody section growing up from the ground. So *cépage* should be understood as "of the stock."

CÉRONS • This sweet white wine appellation from Bordeaux in France was named after a village there, whose name is thought to have come from a Latin personal name. The place name was first seen as *Sirio* in the 4th century.

CHABLIS • These wines are named for a town in Burgundy. *Chablis* appeared first in English in 1668 as *Chablee*. French records indicate the town's name evolved from *Capleia* in 867 to *Chablies* by 1187 and *Chablis* by 1308. Some of these minor variations in spelling have to be taken with a grain of salt, since spelling conventions in French or English didn't completely stabilize until well after all of these dates. The ultimate source of the town's name is unknown, but that hasn't stopped people guessing. One suggestion is some relation to the Latin word *capulum*, which itself has several interpretations, including one roughly equivalent to our English "cable" and another as "a wooden handle." Both senses derive from a sense of "holding" something. There is some suggestion that the word's application to Chablis may have something to do with controlling wood floating on the Serein River, where Chablis is located, but this connection is obscure. There is, coincidentally, another French *chablis*—a word that refers to a tree that has fallen due to wind damage.

CHAIS • Sometimes a French wine cork or label will be printed with the phrase *mis en bouteille dans nos chais*. A little knowledge is a dangerous thing, because the word *chaise* is French for "chair" and that might cause a barely French-speaking drinker to conclude that the wine was "put in bottles in our chairs." However, *chais* is the plural of *chai*, a storage warehouse—usually in Bordeaux—where wine is generally kept in barrels. The value of the phrase *mis en bouteille dans nos chais* is associated with times when wine fraud was widespread and buyers wanted to know that the expensive wine they had purchased had not been substituted or diluted by an unscrupulous trader on its way to their table. If the wine was bottled at the source, such tampering was assumed to be less likely. The word *chai* is thought to be a variant of the French word *quai*, which had been used in the ancient province of Poitou in what is now west-central France. The French word *quai* is closely related to our English word *quay*, meaning "shipping pier." Because such piers were full of activity, the word *quai* was extended to refer also to areas dedicated to loading and unloading goods, including railway platforms. The words are thought to have come not from Latin but instead from the Gaulish word *caio*, which traced its roots even further back to the Celtic word *kagio*.

CHALK HILL • This wine region north of Santa Rosa in California shares the name *Chalk* with roughly 20 other geographic features in the state, all presumably named for chalk-like stone outcroppings. The word *chalk* comes from Old English and evolved from the Germanic of the Anglo-Saxons. Before that, it probably came from the Latin words *calx* or *calcum*, which are also the roots of our English words *calculus* and *calcium*. The Romans likely picked up the word from Greek, where *khalix* meant "pebble." As an English word, *chalk* is recorded in some of the oldest glosses, dating from around the year 700. A gloss is a translation of a single word, and a glossary is a collection of such translations. Old glosses are interesting to etymologists because the first examples of written English didn't appear in the form of sentences, paragraphs or pages. Initially, to help readers understand Latin manuscripts, medieval scholars wrote Old English words between the lines of Latin, or in the page margins. These glosses have survived mostly because they were contained in sacred holy texts that were kept safe in monasteries.

CHALONE • Chalone is a wine region in California named from a native word. The original inhabitants prior to European arrival are now known as the Ohlone or Costaloan people. An 1816 reference to "the Chalone language" supports the contention of some authorities that the *Chalone* was one of the tribal groups within the Ohlone. Other sources extract *Chalone* from the Ohlone word *calon* of unknown meaning. The place name *Chalone* and several spelling variants began appearing on maps in the mid 1800s.

CHAMBOURCIN • Chambourcin is a grape type named for the town of Bouge-Chambalud in the Rhône, where the variety was developed. It was only in 1963 that the grape type began to be marketed. Two years later, its creator Joannès Seyve died at 65, unaware that the variety would be taken up all over the world.

CHAMPAGNE • It is commonly accepted that the area in France so famous for its sparkling wines gained its name in Roman times, when the Latin word *campania* was used to describe the area as an open, rolling landscape. The same word applies to the Campania region in Italy, whence the Romans came. But there are dissenters in every crowd, and a second theory on the name of the French region is that it comes from Celtic *kann pan*, which means "white country," because there are white, chalky outcroppings here and there.

CHARDONNAY • Sources trace the use of the word *Chardonnay* in English back only to 1911, when it appeared in the *Encyclopaedia Britannica*, but the great French *Robert* dictionary identifies *Chardonnay* as a place name. Between the cities of Dijon and Lyon in France, there is a very small village called Chardonnay that is reported to take its name from the Latin word *cardonnacum*. This word likely arose based on the personal name *Cardus*, thought to be Gaulish. However, *carduus* is also the Latin word for "thistle," so some people believe the meaning of *Chardonnay* to be "a place of thistles."

CHASSELAS • A widely planted if not widely revered grape, *Chasselas* is a synonym for Fendant and is a variety with numerous claims on its provenance. Although some approach not only the vine's parentage but also the etymology of the name *Chasselas* with caution, it seems likely that the name came from the name of the village of Chasselas in Mâconnais, France. The village's name is believed to have been based on the personal Latin name *Cacilius*. *Chasselas* as a grape name is seen in the French literature as far back as 1654. The *Fendant* name for the grape goes back even further, to the end of the 16th century. *Fendant* means "splitter," and these grapes split when pressed between two fingers, as opposed to bursting. The *Dictionnaire des noms de cépages de France* points to a third synonym, *Filant*, which highlights the value of this splitting attribute; *Filant* probably meant "juicy, flowing under pressure."

CHÂTEAU • There have been châteaux in France since before the Romans marched home. In Old French the word was *chastel*, from which English got *castle*, but before that came the Latin word *castellum*. On the one hand, this had meant "fortress," but it was also extended to apply to the town or village that surrounded the fortress. A bottle of wine marked with the word *château* may or may not be associated with a large mansion or castle. The prestige associated with the word *château* has influenced its addition to numerous wine names and has also influenced the building of numerous châteaux. But, these days, *château* is also a technical designation relating to a winegrowing property, so some châteaux marked on wine labels may represent properties totally bereft of edifices of any description.

CHÂTEAU AUSONE • This small estate at St-Émilion in France is named for a local boy who made good. His name was Decimius Magnus Ausonius and he lived in the early 300s, when the area was under Roman rule. The fact that his father was said to have been of Greek extraction underlines the fact that non-peasants have long been internationally mobile. Ausonius himself was called to Rome as a tutor to the son of the Emperor. Though he spent much of his life first as a teacher and then as an administrator (a senior one—he was a prefect and a consul), he is remembered as a poet. Some of his most frequently noted poetry transmits his affection for a girl across 17 centuries. She was Bissula, a German slave he won as the spoils of war but freed and clearly loved.

CHÂTEAU CHEVAL BLANC • The *Cheval* of Château Cheval Blanc in Bordeaux is French for "horse" and comes from the Latin *caballus*, which gave English the word *cavalcade*, meaning "a procession of horses."

CHÂTEAU HAUT-BRION • The fame of this Bordeaux wine means that it shows up relatively early in the English written record. Samuel Pepys mentions it as *Ho Bryan* in his diary entry for April 10, 1663, just over 100 years after the Château was established. Pepys tasted the wine at the Royal Oak Tavern on Lombard Street in London and, remarkably, there is another connection between this street and this wine. On April 21, 1886, the Institute of Bankers held one of its regular meetings, at which a member read a report—not a report about banking, but one designed to entertain. The world was a different place back then, and there were fewer entertainments. What passed for an evening of fun was the reading of 30-plus pages of a detailed account of the entire historical record of each address on Lombard Street: which businesses had occupied each address; the names of each proprietor; and the look of the sign that had hung above each door. The reading incited enthusiastic discussion (yawn), and two points in particular relate to our interest in the name of the wine. The diligent researcher of the evening—a man named F. G. Hilton Price—reported that a restaurant called Puntack's Head was established by a Monsieur Pontac of the family that owned Haut-Brion. More specifically, Price reported that the vineyard owners who produced the "choice claret" were Pontac and O'Brien. That stimulated the etymological postulation from the audience that perhaps *Haut-Brion* was a French pronunciation of *O'Brien*. This banker's suggestion has never been taken too seriously by lexicographers. It seems more likely that just as *Puntack* was an English version of *Pontac*, *O'Brien*–like *Ho Bryan*–was an Anglicization of *Haut-Brion*. The French word *haut* evolved from the same Germanic root as the English word *high* and refers to the height of land upon which the vineyard sits. The name *Brion* is harder to trace, and no specific meaning is reported for its use in *Haut-Brion*. Yet the *Dictionnaire étymologique des noms de lieux en France* indicates that *brion* has Gaulish roots that once meant "high place." Such duplication is a bit mysterious, since Haut-Brion isn't all *that* high. The *Dictionnaire* also suggests that, depending on context, *brion* could also mean "situated on a plain."

CHÂTEAU PÉTRUS • Château Pétrus of Pomerol in Bordeaux is named to honor St. Peter, since *Petrus* is Latin for Peter. The winery uses various symbols that relate to St. Peter, such as a boat and fishing net, since Peter was a fisherman before becoming a follower of Christ. The keys depicted on Pétrus labels represent St. Peter's keys to the kingdom of heaven. The Greek root *petros* of the Latin *Petrus* means "rock."

CHÂTEAU D'YQUEM • This is a strange name but a famous one, from Sauternes in Bordeaux; *Yquem* is said to have evolved from the Germanic name or title *aighelm*, which supposedly breaks down as *aigan* and *helm* to mean "to have a helm." These obscure connections are thought to indicate a noble background, as would fit an ancestor who wore a helmet.

CHÂTEAUNEUF-DU-PAPE • This appellation from the Rhône region in France dates from a time when the centre of the Catholic Church was in France, not Italy. In the early 1300s Pope Clement V decided that he liked the thought of living in Avignon better than living in Rome, so the entire papal court pulled up stakes and moved. Of course, the pope needed a new house in the new location, and so Châteauneuf-du-Pape, which means "the Pope's new castle," came to be. Where there are popes, there is wine, and the next pope, John XXII, established a papal vineyard at the site. Though there has been prestige at Châteauneuf-du-Pape for 700 years and the wines of Châteauneuf-du-Pape now carry much prestige, the wine's current reputation only established itself over the past century.

CHEERS • When you lift your glass and say "cheers," what exactly are you saying? You are encouraging your drinking companions to smile. The word *cheer* first appeared in the written English record back around 1225. At that first surfacing, there appear to have been several meanings already attached to the word. On the one hand, someone's cheer was their state of mind; the phrase *be of good cheer* comes from this meaning. But, more fundamentally, their state of mind was expressed in the look on their face, and this look was also called their *cheer*. Both of these meanings came to *cheer* because of its original French meaning, "face," which came from the Old French word *chiere*. Since French had evolved from Latin, it's no surprise that the Romans had a similar word, *cara*. In turn, many Latin words have Greek roots, and in Greek *kara* meant "head" instead of "face." The word root is thought to go even further back into the lost language of Indo-European, where a *ker* was not only a "head" but also a "horn."

CHENIN • A word applied to the grape type Chenin Blanc but also occasionally to Chenin Noir. *The Oxford English Dictionary* not only says that the grape's designation as *Chenin* possibly comes from a particular estate called Mont-Chenin but further speculates that Mont-Chenin takes its name from the Old French word for "dog-like," the Latin *canis* being "dog." The *Dictionnaire des noms de cépages de France* suggests instead that the grape type was named "dog" for its wild origins. First mentioned in French in 1534 by Rabelais, *Chenin* was also included by Randal Cotgrave in his French-English dictionary in 1611. However, since this inclusion was on the French side, *Chenin* isn't actually considered to have been used as an English word until 1896.

CHIANTI • The first unambiguous reference to the Italian wine Chianti appeared in the 13th century, but the first English document known to refer to it dates to 1833. The name of the wine comes from the name of the region in which it is produced in northwest Italy. That first Italian reference described the Chianti Mountains, not vineyards. The origin of *Chianti* is obscure, but the word might have come from the Latin word *clangor*, referring to the sound of hunting horns. A second theory is that an Etruscan family name, *Clante*, might have been the source.

CHILE • Chile is a notable wine-producing country in that it has been successful in giving the cold shoulder to phylloxera. As such, Chilean vines grow naturally on their own roots, unlike most European and North American vines, which must be grafted to phylloxera-resistant rootstocks. There are numerous theories as to the origin of the country's name, but some gain additional appeal from the English homonym *chilly*, meaning "cold"; though *chilly* has no etymological connection to *Chile*. Before the arrival of the Spanish in the 1400s a mix of native peoples populated the long corridor that is now Chile. Words meaning "cold" and "snow" from their various languages have been offered and may have a notional association with the frosty peaks of the Andes Mountains that border Chile to the east. Another suggested native parent word for *Chile* has a meaning of "land's end." Since the country stretches to the extreme southern end of South America—the closest point of any habitable continent to Antarctica—this meaning too has an extended sense of "cold" to it.

CHOCOLATE • Chocolate relates to wine not only because notes of chocolate aroma are sometimes experienced in wine, but also because chocolate has roots as a ceremonial drink that might be compared to wine. We get our English word *chocolate* from Spanish explorers 500 years ago, who found native Central Americans using cacao beans as an ingredient in a drink they held in particularly high esteem. The drink was unsweetened and contained ingredients that gave it a bitter taste. *Chocolate* as a word is thought to be built on the Nahuatl language's words for "bitter" and "water." Archeological evidence suggests that before this drink arose, as early as 3000 years ago, Central Americans were brewing an alcoholic drink from the husks of the cacao seeds. The elaborate ceremony surrounding chocolate as observed by Spanish explorers may have grown up earlier around a kind of cacao-based wine or beer. The theoretical chain of events is that, at some point, people in Central America discovered that the pulp of the seedpods of cacao could ferment and produce an alcoholic beverage. There, just as with wine in the Mediterranean, the desirability of such a drink led to its widespread use and high social value. Pottery shards containing traces of telltale cacao constituents appear to be pieces of the "best dishes" used for special occasions. Since the flavors we associate with chocolate do not develop if the

50

cacao beans are not fermented, it is suspected that chocolate as we know it emerged later, possibly as an accidental by-product of this cacao wine production. The social and ceremonial protocols for drinking chocolate observed by Spanish explorers may have arisen based on an earlier alcoholic drink.

CHOPINE • A chopine or chopin is a wine bottle of diminutive size, imprecise volume, and uncertain etymology. Differing sources provide volumes ranging from 250 milliliters, or one third of a standard bottle, to more than two thirds. The word may have come to English from French—and, if so, may be from another vessel called a *chope*—but it is also associated with the German word *schoppen*, which translates as "pint" but is etymologically built on the same root as *scoop*. A pint itself ranges from between 473 milliliters and 568 milliliters, depending which side of the Atlantic it is on. Despite the imprecision of the measure, English drinkers certainly knew what the word stood for, because the verb *chopin* evolved, meaning "to drink," surviving as a word for more than 400 years over the middle of the last millennium.

CINSAUT and CINSAULT • Louis Bouschet first mentioned this grape variety in French in 1829 as *sinsâou*, in an article describing several varieties of grapes. The article appeared in a bulletin of the agricultural society of the department de l'Hérault, on the Mediterranean coast of France. *The Oxford English Dictionary* reports French spellings as widely varied as *cinq-saou* but dates the word's appearance in English, as *Cinsaut*, only to 1945. The meaning of the name has been lost, but it is believed that it was originally used in Languedoc.

CLARE VALLEY • This winegrowing region of Australia takes its name from the local town of Clare, founded by Edward Gleeson in the 1840s and named for County Clare in Ireland. Before acquiring the name Clare, the Australian settlement had been called *Inchiquin, Gleeson's Village,* and *The Twins* for two gum trees that grew there. *Inchiquin*, like *Clare*, harkened back to Ireland, since *Inchiquin* was the title of a barony. County Clare is named for a Gaelic word meaning "board" or "plank." While one source says that is due to the flatness of the landscape there, another source traces the name to a plank bridge that spanned the Fergus River at the Irish town of Clare.

CLARET • Whereas, in England, the wine from Bordeaux referred to as *claret* is considered extra special, in North America, *claret* hardly appears in a wine lover's vocabulary. This variation across continents is matched by a variation in the word's meaning across centuries. *Claret* evolved through French from the Latin word for "clear." Yet the proud reds of Bordeaux are deep and dark—anything but clear. It was their forerunners in the Middle Ages that gave them the name *claret*. The word showed up in French in the 12th century as *clairet* and in English around 1400. At first, it was used to distinguish certain wines from those that were clearly red or white. Claret was somewhere in between, perhaps what we'd call *rosé* today. By about the time of Shakespeare, the meaning had shifted to the red end of the spectrum and has stayed there ever since. Along with the English word *claret*, there has existed since 1450 a grape type called *clairette*, *clarette*, or *claret* in French, due to its light color.

CLARKSBURG • The California town of Clarksburg was founded in 1849 during the gold rush and named for Robert C. Clark, a judge from Ohio reported to be the first to grow peaches in the area of Clarksburg.

CLAVELIN • A clavelin is a slightly smaller-than-standard bottle used for a unique French wine called *vin jaune*, meaning "yellow wine." The volume is 620 milliliters and theoretically represents the volume of wine remaining after a full liter of wine is aged for six years in wood. The origin of the bottle name is uncertain but it may come from *clavus*, the

Latin word for "nail" or "peg." This Latin word is certainly the root of the spice we know as *cloves*, whose shape is perhaps more nail-like than that of the slightly stubby clavelin bottle.

CLEAR LAKE • California's Clear Lake, which has lent its name to the local winegrowing region, was earlier called *Laguna Grande* by Spanish explorers. It was renamed *Clear Lake* by 1851, when it was noted prominently in the journal of George Gibbs, who was acting as a native language interpreter on an expedition to draw up land treaties with the local Indians. He evidently didn't speak the language of the *Clear Lake Indians*, as he calls them, and he makes no mention of any alternative names for the place.

CLINTON • This American grape type was a spontaneous variety—that is, one not developed by a breeder—and was discovered by Hugh White in 1819. The *Dictionnaire des noms de cépages de France* suggests that the grape was named in honor of De Witt Clinton, who served as mayor of New York City and governor of New York State, and made an unsuccessful run for president of the United States. If the date of the discovery of the Clinton vine is accurate, then it represents a period of the politician's life when he was suffering political rejection. That may be a fitting parallel to the grape's career, since it was initially welcomed due to its phylloxera resistance and then rejected due to its foxy flavor.

CLONE • In 1996, Dolly the sheep made headlines because she had been cloned from her "mother." As you already know, that means that instead of being conceived by the usual means involving a ram and a ewe, she was grown entirely from a single mammary cell and, as such, had a set of genetic blueprints identical to her mother's. Dolly made headlines because she was a technological and scientific breakthrough with many implications in the fields of health and ethics. But to vintners, the idea of cloning was old hat. To reproduce an animal by cloning requires delicate manipulations at a cellular level. To reproduce a vine by cloning only requires snipping off a twig and getting the thing to sprout new roots and leaves, something it wants to do anyway. There are two consequences to this fact, although they are certainly less earth shattering than Dolly's implications. One is that, all over the world, vineyards are populated with vines that have been reproduced asexually. As a result, the genetic variation across a number of plants in a vineyard is orders of magnitude lower than the genetic variation across a patch of grass on a golf course with the same number of individual plants. That is both amazing and a little scary. The second consequence of the ease of vine cloning is that the etymology of *clone* comes from very near the vineyard. *Clone* comes from the Greek word *klon*, meaning "twig." The word first appeared in English in 1903 and referred only to the asexual reproduction of plants. It was futurist Alvin Toffler who first applied the word to the potential cloning of people in 1970. Yet according to *Collins Dictionaries*, in their list of 100 words that define the 20th century, *clone* didn't emerge in the popular consciousness until 1992.

CLOS • Wines that have the word *clos* on their label are making the claim that they have been grown in a vineyard surrounded by a wall. Clos de Vougeot is a famous example and was first referred to by an English wine writer in 1793. The word *clos* simply means "enclosed" and goes back in French to the 12th century. Walls were certainly being built around vineyards by the 1300s, as was the case for Clos de Vougeot, so it's likely vineyards were also walled before that. Walls serve the triple purpose of elevating the stature of a property, keeping roaming domestic animals or wildlife from helping themselves, and reducing losses due to hungry peasants. The etymology of *clos* is the Latin *claudere* and is related to the Latin *clavis* meaning "bar" or "key." *Clavis* gave doctors the name of the bone at the top of your chest, the clavicle, and also gave French the word *clé*, meaning "key."

Although *key* and *clé* have similar sounds and meaning, etymologists have not established a link between the two words. *Key* developed from Old English and is not widely distributed in other Germanic languages.

COCKTAIL • Why should a mixed drink be called a *cocktail?* The short answer is that nobody knows. The long answer is that the word *cocktail* referred first to horses whose owners had clipped short their tails in order to make them stand up as a rooster's tail would; thus, a *cock's tail.* Although the expression is thought to have been used verbally earlier, the first written examples of this use date to 1808. Mixed drinks being called *cocktails* appear in writing in 1803 but this name would not have arisen out of thin air. No one has been able to establish whether there is any connection between the two uses, nor establish an unassailable theory as to why mixed drinks might have taken on the name. But that doesn't stop us speculating. The horses with clipped tails that were called *cocktails* were usually not purebreds. Thus, the idea that they were a mixture could have something to do with the name of a drink mixture. Another theory is based on the fact that the first two citations for *cocktail* as "a drink," as found in *The Oxford English Dictionary,* refer unambiguously to *cocktail* as a "pick-me-up" or "stimulant." The image of a raised tail goes well with perkiness, and that may tie into the choice of the name for such drinks.

COFFEE • Not only is coffee a valuable commodity for someone who has enjoyed wine the night before, but the etymology of the word *coffee* may be tied to wine as well. Coffee, the drink, landed on Europe in the 1600s. The word is believed to have come from Arabic, although English may have gotten it through the intermediary of Italian. Beyond Arabic, the etymology gets hazy. Arabic lexicographers have theorized that the word originally designated a type of wine and came from the root word *qahiya,* meaning "to be without appetite." That is by no means certain. Other theories include the tracing of *coffee* back to an area called Kaffa in Ethiopia, where the bean may have first grown wild.

COLE RANCH • Cole Ranch is an officially recognized American Viticultural Area (AVA) in Mendocino County, California, and is unusual in at least three ways. Named after a man still living, John Cole, it is also the smallest AVA on the books. Although he applied for and gained the AVA designation, John Cole didn't actually name the site. After buying the property in 1971, he turned it to vines—himself a first time wine grower. He sold his first crop in 1975 to winery Château St. Jean, which, without Cole's knowledge, labeled the resulting bottles with the designation *Cole Ranch.*

COLLI ALBANI • *Colli Albani* literally means "Alban Hills" and is the name of one of the wines from the Italian Castelli Romani region southeast of Rome. The Alban hills rise above the Castelli Romani region and may be named from the pre-Celtic word *alb,* meaning "hill." The words *colli* and *colline* are applied to a number of other hilly wine areas in Italy from the Latin word for "hill," *collis.*

COLOMBARD • A white grape named for its color, *Colombard* is seen in citations dating back as far as 1706. In French *colombe,* from the Latin word *colomba,* means "dove." Beyond the literal meaning of "dove," the word *colombe* holds a sense of softness and purity in French, though these attributes may or may not have been applied to the wine.

CONCORD • Concord grapes are not highly thought of in the world of wine. They are named after the city of Concord, Massachusetts. Figuratively, the word *concord* means "of one mind," from its Latin roots *con* ("together") and *cord* ("heart"). However, the name is at odds with the experience of Ephraim Bull, the grape's first promoter. Bull developed the strain of grapes to survive the climate in New England and then sold his crop, as would any other farm producer. But he also sold vine cuttings, and his neighbors built up production capacity that eventually undercut his market. His grave is marked with the epitaph, "He Sowed Others Reaped."

CONNOISSEUR • *The Devil's Dictionary* by Ambrose Bierce was published in 1911 and within its definition for *connoisseur* was the following example: *An old wine-bibber having been smashed in a railway collision, some wine was poured on his lips to revive him. "Pauillac, 1873," he murmured and died.* The word *connoisseur* came into English 300 years ago with a meaning of "one who knows." Before reaching English, it had been French, with roots through Latin and Greek right back to Indo-European, where *gno-* is at the heart of such "knowing" words as *cunning, incognito, recognize,* and *reconnaissance.* It was just over 200 years ago that *connoisseur* was applied as a word in English meaning someone who appreciates wines through an extensive knowledge of them. Connoisseurship must have had a rocky start, because the first known citation expresses admiration by those supposed connoisseurs for crabapple cider.

CONSTELLATION • The name of the world's largest wine company appropriately means "all the stars together," from Latin *con* or *com,* meaning "together," and *stella,* meaning "star." The word *star* represents something that people have been looking up at and talking about for all of human history. It's no surprise that this word goes back 8000 years or more to the Indo-European *ster.*

COONAWARRA • This winegrowing area in South Australia was named from an Aboriginal word (or words) meaning "honeysuckle" or "honeysuckle on a hillside."

COOPER • The family name Cooper refers to some ancestor who was a craftsman specializing in the construction of wooden barrels. In English, this professional title didn't appear until the 14th century. It seems to have come from a Germanic source and, before that, probably from a Latin word for "cask." However, there were already related words in English. A chicken coop is called a *coop* because *coop* was an old word for a wicker basket and, later, a cage. That's why we sometimes use the expression *feeling cooped up*. In English, a barrel was never called a *coop*, even though the folks who made them were called *coopers*.

CORBIERES • This French winegrowing area, near the spot where France abuts both Spain and the Mediterranean, is said by some to take its name from a place where crows gather. The logic is that the French word for "crow" is *corbeau* from the Latin *corvus*, meaning "raven." However, this is likely a folk etymology. Adrian Room's *Placenames of France* offers instead the pre-Indo-European root *kor*, a variant of *kar*, meaning "rock" or "mountain." That would be appropriate for a region at the edge of the Pyrenees.

CORK • When we hear the word *cork*, we think first of the stopper in a wine bottle. The same material has been used for thousands of years for similar purposes, but the word would not have evoked this image until around 300 years ago. There are classical references to the use of cork to seal amphora (those ancient two-handled wine jars), but between then and the 17th century, most wine containers—such as casks or skin bags—didn't lend themselves to being sealed with a cork. It wasn't until the 1600s that glass bottles came into wide use for storing wine, and corks only became a common closure after that time. Cork is the outer bark of a particular type of oak tree with the scientific Latin name *Quercus suber*. *Quercus* is the Latin word for "oak," usually the kind that produces acorns; *suber* is the Latin word for the particular kind of oak that produces cork. Some think that the similarity in sound between *quercus* and *cork* is not an accident and that the word *cork* arose from *quercus*. But another potential candidate for the etymology of *cork* relates to the tree's bark. One part of our brains is called the *cortex*, named because it wraps around the rest of the brain like the outer surface of a tree; *cortex* is the Latin word for "bark." So it is also possible that cork is called *cork* because it comes from the bark or *cortex* of the *quercus* tree. The first references in English to *cork* predated bottle stoppers and referred instead to shoes made with cork soles. This reference likely came from Spain, where the Spanish word for cork, *corche*, appears to have grown out of an Arabic word also referring to cork footwear; the southern part of Spain was under Muslim control for about 700 years before the 1400s. Besides the fact that bottles hadn't been invented yet, a Muslim source of the word would likely not have emphasized a use related to wine. But the Arabic word could have easily come from one of the two Latin roots mentioned above, because this part of the world—Spain and Portugal—is exactly the place where *Quercus suber* trees grow naturally. Arriving Muslim conquerors would likely have adopted the local word for the tree. Even earlier, the Latin root of *quercus* evolved from the Indo-European root *perkwu*, also meaning "oak," and *cortex* from another Indo-European root, *sker* or *ker*, meaning "to cut," so that the *cortex* or bark is the part of the tree that "can be cut away." Finally, the Latin name for the cork oak, *suber*, may also derive from its bark; the extended meaning of *suber* is "tree with wrinkled bark" and may relate to a Greek word for "wrinkled skin."

CORKSCREW • Before wine was stored in bottles, there was little need for corkscrews. Before consensus named the device a *corkscrew*, it suffered under the alternate names *worm* and *bottle-screw*. A *worm* for cork extraction is cited as early as 1681. The tool is called a *corkscrew* as early as 1720 but as recently as 1938 is cited as a *bottle-screw*. The word *screw* first shows up in English in 1404 from French, but in French the word applied not to what you might think of as a screw but instead to the female equivalent, now more conventionally called a *nut*. Sources tie the French word back to a Latin word for a female pig. One theory is that perhaps the curly tail of the pig might have influenced the naming of a similarly twisting piece of hardware. Another Latin word might also have influenced the naming of the screw; this Latin word meant "ditch" or "trench" and might have been applied to the slot in the top of the screw or, some say, to the gap between threads of the screw. This theory still ties in with the pig etymology, because the "ditch" meaning may relate to a pig rooting in the soil and cutting a trench. Although a worm may also cut through soil, the etymology of the word *worm* wriggled in from another direction. There is a guttural feel to the word that comes from its Old English ancestry. When *worm* first arose in English, it referred not to the creatures sometimes skewered on fishhooks but to snakes and dragons. J. R. R. Tolkien was historically accurate in calling a dragon a *worm*. This word has a long enough history that its roots in Indo-European sprouted parallel words through Germanic and Latin. The Germanic and Old English gave us *worm*; the Latin gave us *vermin*.

CORSICA • This French island off the knee of Italy's boot is likely one of the oldest wine-producing regions in Europe. Its name is of uncertain origin. One theory is that *Corsica* comes from the Phoenician word *horsi,* meaning "wooded," due to the belief that Phoenician boats were built of Corsican pine. A rival theory is that it is based on a Latinate personal name.

CÔTE OR COTEAUX • This is a prefix to numerous place names in France, such as Côte d'Or. These words mean "side" or "hillside." They are closely related to our word *coast,* meaning "seaside." They evolved from the Latin word *costa,* which meant "side" as well but also meant "rib," such as the ones in your side. The Indo-European root may have been *kost,* meaning "bone."

CÔTE CHALONNAISE • This wine region in Burgundy takes its name from the city of Chalon-sur-Saône, a place Julius Caesar called *Cabillinum*. The Latin name may have in turn been based on the earlier Ligurian word root *cab*, meaning "height."

CÔTE D'OR • An extremely important area of Burgundy, *Côte d'Or* literally translates as "golden side." In this case, *côte* (meaning "side") is applied to a series of hillsides along the escarpment stretching south-southwest of Dijon. The word *or* means "gold" and its etymology is the Latin *aurum*, also meaning "gold"; that is also the root from which El Dorado, the mythical land of gold, was spun. The Côte d'Or has certainly earned a lot of riches over the centuries, and the name may relate to the color of the grapevines with a nod to their high quality, but there is an alternative theory on the origin of the region's name. The hillsides where grapes are grown face east. The sun rises in the east, and the Latin word for "rise" was *oriri*. This Latin root gave both French and English the word *orient*, meaning "east." In English, *the Orient* is a slightly dated phrase referring to countries in the Far East; *to orient* something means to turn it a certain way, but originally it meant explicitly "to turn toward the east." So *Côte d'Or* may quite possibly be a contraction of *Côte d'Orient*.

COTEAUX D'AIX-EN-PROVENCE • In 123 BCE, the Romans founded a military fortress at this place in the southeast corner of France. They named it after both a geothermal spring they found there and the Roman proconsul in charge. His name was Sextius Calvinus, but that part of the place name has been dropped over the millennia. Geothermal springs however, are still known as *waters*, and back in Latin the word for *waters* was *aquae*. The same forces that washed the Roman proconsul off the city's name shrank *Aquae* down to *Aix*. The latter part of the modern name

61

applies to the region of Provence, of which Aix is the capital. (See **Provence**, p. 140.)

CÔTES DE CASTILLON • The Côtes de Castillon appellation contrôlée in Bordeaux takes its name from the town of Castillon-la-Bataille. *Castillon* means "castle" and *bataille* means "battle." There are many places in France named for castles and this one had previously been known as *Castillon-sur-Dordogne*, Dordogne being the river upon which it is located. But in 1953, the town's name was changed to commemorate a 1453 battle during the Hundred Years' War—the war during which Joan of Arc rose and fell. The Battle of Castillon was the final battle of the war and the one that marked the end of English rule in what we now think of as France. (See **château**, p. 45, and **Dordogne**, p. 68.)

CRÉMANT • The term *crémant* is used to designate good French sparkling wine that isn't from the region of Champagne. The term has an etymology that is a little less bubbly but just as heady. In English, we use an almost identical word, *creamy*, to describe the foam that forms on some glasses of beer. These words are easy to associate with *cream*. It is the oil or fat in cream that gives it its name, from the French word *crème*, which arose from the Latin *chrism*. But *chrism* did not refer to the fatty part of milk, instead it was a church word for the oil used in anointing. This word in turn came from the Greek word for "anoint," and if *chrism* looks a little like the word *Christ*, that's because *Christ* means "anointed" in Greek.

CROATIA • Wine has been produced for at least 2000 years in what is now Croatia. The country's name is of Slavic origin and is thought to be related to the Russian word *khrebet*, which means "mountain chain." That is appropriate, as the Kapela and Velebit ranges stand here between the Lika Plateau and the Adriatic.

CRU • Some very fine wines have this little word *cru* on the label. It is a French word that comes from the past participle of the French word *croître,* meaning "to grow." Most English translations peg *cru* as "growth"; *premier crus* are thus "first growths." But that only tells part of the story; more might be told by analogy. Referring to people as having "good breeding" can mean the genetic stock they came from, but more likely refers to their upbringing. It's like that for wines too. Certainly, respected *crus* must use classier grape varieties, but what is just as important to their ultimate success is their upbringing: the soil, the sun, the rain, the way they were tended, and the way they were guided to their public debut.

CRUSH • Sighs might be the only sound you would associate with a teenager who has a crush on someone. The sounds of crushing grapes are similarly subtle, so much so that the noise from the crusher mechanism might be expected to drown out most of the sounds of bursting grape skins and flowing juice. Yet when the word *crush* first popped into English out of the French of the Norman Conquest, there was as much a sense of sound to the word as there was violent action. That obsolete meaning is expressed in *The Oxford English Dictionary* as "the sound of violent percussion, to clash, crash; to make the harsh grating noise of things forcibly smashed or pounded to fragments." This sense of acoustic violence also existed in the French predecessor word and its parent words in Germanic. The sound died away in English after the 1400s, leaving only the physical compression element. Like many words, *crush* has adopted other meanings, of course, such as the sense of "teenage love" that appeared first in America in the late 1800s. Another meaning that relates to wine (and love) shows up in *Romeo and Juliet.* In Shakespeare's play, a servant of Juliet's father invites Romeo—if he is not a Montague (but he is)—to "crush a cup of wine" up at the Capulet place. By that he means come and "enjoy" a glass.

CULTIVAR • The Latin word *cultivare* means "to till," and it gave English the word *cultivate* in the early 1600s. A *cultivar* is a plant variety that has come into being due to human efforts in cultivation. The word *cultivar* had to wait until 1923 to sprout from the pen of Liberty Hyde Bailey, a pioneer in agriculture who brought together horticulture and botany. Before Bailey, no one seemed to suppose that the study of growing crops might benefit from knowledge of the science of plants. Among his many innovations, Bailey was influential in starting the American youth movement called the 4-H Club.

CUVÉE • Since most English-speaking wine buyers don't know what *cuvée* means, it adds a little mystery and prestige to a wine label. The word derives from another French word *cuve*, which simply means "vat." Until recently, most vats were constructed out of wood, so it makes sense that the French word *cuve* evolved from the Latin word *cupe*, which meant "cask." What is a wooden vat but an overgrown cask? This Latin word root is also related to *cooper*, the professional title of a cask builder, and also to *cup*, a cup being a teeny-tiny cask.

CYPRUS • Although not a wine power now, Cyprus was once at the very center of the wine world. The island's name is believed to have come from the Sumerian word *kabar* or *gabar*, which the Greeks adopted as *Kupros* to describe the copper resources once mined there. The English word *copper* derives from this same root.

D

DAVIS • The name of the city where it is located is often used as an abbreviation for the full title of an important viticultural education and research center, the California State University at Davis. The city was earlier known as Davisville after the successful farm enterprise of Jerome C. Davis, who arrived in the area in the early 1850s. Mr. Davis earned considerable wealth by serving those who came seeking California gold but experienced tragedy too. His only child died in an accident at his mill, and drought in the late 1860s forced the sale of the farm.

DECANTER • There are two theories as to the etymology of *decanter*. It clearly is named because one decants from it. But *decant* may come from *cant*, meaning "to be on edge" or "to lean." Or, according to a more popular theory, it may originate from the fact that the spout of a decanter was likened to the corner of the human eye, which in Greek was called *kanthos*.

DEMI-SEC • A French term meaning "medium dry" when referring to the sweetness of a wine. The prefix *demi-* is common in English and came into the language in the 1400s from French, which got it from Latin. The Latin root is appropriate to the "medium dry" meaning because the source is two Latin words, *dis medius*, which literally meant "divided in half." *Demi* is also a term used to describe a bottle that is half the standard size. *Sec,* also French, comes from the Latin word *siccus*, meaning "dry", which is also the source of the English word *desiccate*.

DESSERT • Dessert wines are often sweet wines that complement the final course of a meal. The word *dessert* originates in French and derives from the activity that takes place at the table when dessert is about to be enjoyed. The

French word meant "the removal of dishes" and grew out of *desservir*–literally, "un serve." The first time the word *dessert* appeared in English was in 1600 in a book called *Naturall and Artificiall Directions for Health* by one William Vaughan. Not only was Vaughan an enthusiast in the use of the letter "l"; he was also a big booster of the colonization of Newfoundland. He wasn't too keen on dessert, however, calling such "French eating" "unnaturall."

DIESEL • *Diesel* is a term used on the aroma wheel, a wine-tasting tool. Steer away from wines that smell like diesel, sez I. The term is taken from the scent of the type of oil used in diesel engines. Diesel engines are named for their inventor, Rudolf Diesel, an international man from over a century ago. Born in Paris of German parents, he also lived in England, off and on. He died mysteriously, drowning in the English Channel during a ferry crossing in 1913. Some suspected suicide; others suspected murder with international political overtones (World War I began within a year of his death).

DIONYSUS • Dionysus was the Greek forerunner of Bacchus, god of wine. The name Dionysus breaks down into two Greek roots, *dios* and *nyssos*. *Dios* meant "heavenly" in Greek but in this context it more exactly meant the boss in heaven: Zeus. *Dios* is also the root of our word *deity*. *Nyssos* is said to mean "youth" or "son," so that *Dionysus* literally means "son of Zeus," which is appropriate, since the mythology holds Dionysus to be the offspring of Zeus and either Semele or Persephone. Other theories on the latter half of the name exist, but they are not so neat and tidy. Nysa is also said to have been a water nymph (or the Nysiads, a group of nymphs) who nursed the baby Dionysus.

DISGORGEMENT • The removal of spent yeast that has settled in the neck of a bottle of naturally sparkling wine gains its name from the fact that in French the throat is called the *gorge*. Thus, *disgorgement* is literally "removal from the throat." The French word emerged from Latin, possibly a word *gorga* or *gurga*, but there is disagreement on an earlier source. Some suggest an older Latin word, *gurges*, meaning "whirlpool" or "abyss."

DISTILLATION • Before the technology of distillation was widespread, the active ingredient in wine and beer was a mystery. Whiskey, gin, and other distilled liquors are produced by the magic of distillation, because it is lucky chance that alcohol turns from a liquid to a gas at a lower temperature than water does; pure alcohol boils at 79°C and pure water at 100°C. A still does the tricky job of both bringing the alcohol to a boil and condensing it back into a liquid after it's been separated from most of the rest of the brew it started in. The word *distill* comes from the drops of alcohol that reform for collection. The Latin *de stillare* means "to drip down," from *stilla*, meaning "drip."

DOLCETTO • This Italian grape variety's name means "little sweet one," being the diminutive of *dolce*. The Latin root *dulcis* also gave English the word *dulcet*, as in "the dulcet sound of your voice."

DOM PERIGNON • The well-known brand of Champagne was named after its supposed inventor, Pierre Perignon. *Dom* was a title given to Benedictine monks by the Roman Catholic Church of Dom Perignon's day. In 1668, he joined the Abbey of Hautvillers, becoming treasurer and cellar master. His title *Dom* evolved from the Latin *dominus*, meaning "master" or "lord"; his given name, Pierre, means "rock." Although he did contribute greatly to fine winemaking during his lifetime, he didn't "invent" champagne. For example, six years before Dom Perignon took up his post at Hautvillers, Englishman Christopher Merrett presented a paper to the Royal Society in London exploring how adding sugar to wine could produce a secondary fermentation to make sparkling wine. This presentation took place more than 50 years before the first known French documents describing the process. Merrett did not end his days as happily as Dom Perignon, however. As keeper of the library of the College of Physicians, he lost his job after the place burned down in the Great Fire of London. Then he lost his membership in the Royal Society because he couldn't pay his dues.

DOMAINE • French wines are often marked *mis en bouteille au domaine*, or "bottled on the estate," from which it is clear that *domaine* is French for "estate." The word usually refers to an estate in Burgundy and derives from the Latin word *dominus*, the same source that gave Pierre Perignon his title *Dom*. *Dominus* in turn traces its roots deep into history to an Indo-European word, *dem*, meaning "house" or "dwelling." (See **chais**, p. 43.)

DORDOGNE • From east to west and into Bordeaux runs the Dordogne River, named from the ancient Indo-European words *dor*, meaning "stream" or "river," and *anun*, meaning "deep."

DOURO • The Douro wine region in Portugal is named after the Douro River, which takes its name from an ancient Indo-European word for "river," *dor*. The Douro River flows through Portugal but actually starts in Spain at a point closer to the French border than to Portugal's.

DOUX • This French term literally means "sweet" and comes from a Latin word with the same meaning, *dulcis*. (See **dolcetto**, p. 67.)

DOZEN • A case of wine usually holds a dozen bottles. The word *dozen* came into English from French in the year 1300 or so. This is the usual time lag for a word arriving with the French conquerors of 1066 before being be adopted by English speakers and finally set to paper. The Romans had earlier imposed the Latin root word *duodecim* on the Franks and the Gauls. The Latin word breaks down to two words, *duo* and *decem*, meaning "2" and "10," respectively; 2 plus 10 equals a dozen. Both *duo* and *decem* trace their respective roots back to the ancient Indo-European language.

DRINK • *Drink* has been an English word as long as the language has been around in any form that might be referred to as English. It is one of the words that the Anglo-Saxons brought with them when they arrived from what is now Germany, Holland, and northeastern France and filled the power vacuum left by the retreating Romans just over 1500 years ago. This makes it an Old English word, and Old English has Germanic parentage. There are similar words in other Germanic languages but not in other language families. The earliest surviving document known to contain *drincas*, the Old English predecessor word of *drink*, dates from around the year 888. This first example did not refer to an alcoholic drink; the first such use of the word occurs in 1042, 24 years before the Norman Conquest. The 888 document is a translation into English attributed to King Alfred the Great and is known as Boethius' *Consolation of Philosophy*. Poor Boethius had been a high government official in Rome in the early 6th century but had somehow run afoul of the emperor and been condemned to death. As he awaited execution in his cell, he wrote about good and evil in the world and the possibility of happiness even in times of trouble.

DRY CREEK VALLEY • There are more than 100 places named *Dry Creek* in California. Like the Dry Creek of the Dry Creek Valley wine region, most of them must have been named during the dry season, because although water may not be abundant, there is indeed water in many of these creeks some or most of the time. The word *creek* took on a new meaning when it came to North America from England. Originally, it had described a snug bay or secluded curve of water. Europeans explored much of North America by following waterways. It is supposed that as the waterways revealed themselves to English-speaking explorers, some of the features that appeared at first to be "snug bays" proved upon further inspection to be streams. The term *creek* could thus have been extended to this new meaning, eventually losing its original sense.

DUTY • Taxes and duties often make up a substantial part of the cost of a bottle of wine. The word *duty* appeared in this sense in English in 1474 from the presses of the first English printer, William Caxton. It simply means "what is due" and had been used as early as 1297 in other senses that you would still recognize. *Duty* is a special word because, although its root *due* comes from French and Latin, the word *duty* was cooked up in Anglo-French after the conquest of 1066 and isn't found in continental French.

E

EDEN VALLEY • The folk history of the Eden Valley in Australia is that early surveyors found a tree with the word *eden* carved into the bark and so named the valley. The area was first settled around the 1850s. The obvious source of the name is the biblical Garden of Eden. There is no exact spot known to have once been the original Garden of Eden, but the general area where such an earthly paradise might have found its origin was in eastern Mesopotamia. Two theories exist as to the etymology of the *eden* of garden fame. One is that *eden* was a Hebrew word meaning "delight" and that the garden was named based on its occupants' state of bliss. The other theory is that it comes from the Addadian word *edinu,* meaning "plain," describing the landscape of the location. With respect to the Australian *Eden Valley,* if the carved tree theory doesn't satisfy you, it is also true that there are a couple of other places called *Eden* in Australia that were named after George Eden, First Earl of Auckland, who was a senior official in the British government at the time. There are also wineries in California with *Eden* in their names: the Villa Mt. Eden in Napa and the more elevated Mount Eden Vineyards in the Santa Cruz Mountains.

EDNA VALLEY • This small California winegrowing area relates to Lynferd Maxwell, who opened the first post office there in 1887. The post office closed after about 30 years, but a small town was established on the site. At first it was called Maxwellton, but the name quickly reverted to Edna. There are two suggestions as to who the Edna might have been whose name remains affixed to wine labels and what is now only a crossroads. One is that Edna was Lynferd Maxwell's granddaughter. That seems the more likely supposition. The other is a claim made by one Edna Laurel Clark Calhan, that her dad Charles Clark suggested the name.

EGYPT • It is thought that there was a wine trade into Egypt as early as 5000 years ago. There is strong evidence that Egypt's historical elite held wine in extremely high regard, storing wine according to vintage and vineyard millennia earlier than we began to do so in western societies. The ancient city of Memphis in Egypt gave its name to Memphis, Tennessee, both cities being located on great rivers above important deltas. Memphis, Egypt, worshiped the god Ptah, the god of creation. You can hear his godly name at the end of the word *Egypt.* The name *Memphis* means "his beauty" and was a tribute to the supposedly lovely pharaoh Pepi I. But another name for the city was *hut-ka-ptah,* which meant "the temple of the soul of Ptah." After the demise of the power of the pharaohs came the rise of the Greeks, who adopted the name *hut-ka-ptah* in the form of *Aguptos.* They also extended the name to apply beyond city limits to the entire region. As with the pharaohs before them, the Greeks' power faded, this time to be replaced by the Roman Empire. The Greek *Aguptos* thus became *Aegyptus.* We English speakers then took the name of *Egypt* from the Latin of the Bible. All the while, the people who actually lived in Egypt were calling the place *Kemet,* which means "black country." Perhaps this was because the soil of the delta was particularly dark and rich, or else because Egypt was previously inhabited predominantly by dark-skinned Africans.

EL DORADO • This California wine region in the Sierra foothills is named from legend and hope. In the early 1500s, the Spanish conquerors of Central and South America began to relate tales of a fabled Indian chief who, when performing religious rites, appeared completely covered in gold. He was therefore called "the gilded one" or *El Dorado.* The Spanish word *or,* meaning "gold," evolved out of the Classical Latin *aurum.* Clearly, a place where such riches were to be had was a desirable place in general, and the myth of a utopia named *El Dorado* grew. When the gold rush began in California, a mapmaker named Charles Preuss added the name to the area now designated as an American Viticultural Area.

EMILIA-ROMAGNA • This north-central Italian wine region has a double-barreled name for two historical reasons. In 187 BCE, the Roman road known as *Via Aemilia* was established across the region. The road took its name from the Roman consul in charge at the time, Marcus Aemilius Lepidus. The road then lent its name as *Emilia* to the region. Almost 950 years later, in 755, Pippin III, king of the Franks, wrestled five cities in the region from the control of the Lombard ruler Aistulf and handed their rule over to Pope Stephen II. With their control by Rome came the name Romagna. It wasn't until 1948 until the combined name Emilia-Romagna was applied to the region.

ENGUSTMENT • This word refers to the phase of grape growing during which the berries begin to take on flavor and aroma. This technical term only appeared within the last few decades and is not widely used outside of grape growing. As such, lexicographers have not had sufficient time or the pressure of common usage that would induce them to include the word in their dictionaries. The etymology is self-evident, however; since the Latin *gustare* means "to taste," this new term is intended to mean "to fill with taste." The Latin word is believed to have evolved from an Indo-European word, *geus*, also meaning "taste."

ENOPHILE • This playful name for a wine lover literally means "wine lover," based on the Greek *oeno* (meaning "wine") and *phylos* (meaning "loving"). It appears both as *enophile* and *oenophile*, though the leading "o" is silent. The Greek roots are ancient but as an English word, *oenophile* (which appeared first) isn't seen before 1930. It had appeared in French approximately 100 years earlier, but English had at first opted for *oenophilist*. That word was coined by William Makepeace Thackeray, who asked in 1859, "Are the temperance men to be allowed to shout in the public places? [A]re the Vegetarians to bellow "Cabbage for ever"? [A]nd may we modest Oenophilists not sing the praises of our favourite plant?"

ENTRE-DEUX-MERS • Even though the name of this area of Bordeaux is usually translated as "between two seas," it is actually located between two rivers. The answer to the confusion lies in the fact that the Romans called this area *inter duo maria*, which is said to actually have meant *entre deux marées*. The word *marées* in French means "tides," and the tidal bore sweeps up these rivers and around either side of Entre-Deux-Mers; thus, "between two tides." A Google image search on "tidal bore" plus "Dordogne" or "Gironde" (the two rivers bracketing Entre-Deux-Mers) will bring up photos of surfers riding the waves created by these tides.

ESTATE • The interpretation of the word *estate* in the wine world generally relates to a winegrowing property. But the word didn't start out applying to a stretch of turf. The word *estate* is grounded in the same Latin root as the word *state*. Even though a state (meaning a "nation") is an even larger stretch of turf, both words grew out of *status*, which in Latin meant "way of standing," "condition," or "position." Before Latin, the root goes back to the Indo-European *sta*, meaning "to stand." French brought *estate's* parent *estat* to English in the early 1200s, at which time it still meant "condition." But it also already meant "condition in relation to others," which is more like the modern English meaning of *status*. It wasn't until the 1500s that the "status" sense of *estate* began to be attached to possessions that might proclaim one's status. It was the later 1700s before this meaning was transferred specifically to land holdings. Since then, the "land holding" meaning has come to predominate.

ETHANOL • The same chemical that is being added to fossil fuels to make cars more environmentally friendly (successfully or not) gives wine and other alcoholic beverages their kick (rather more successfully). *Ethanol* is a contraction of *ethyl-alcohol* and in turn *ethyl* is a modification of *ether*. The ancestor of all of these words is a Greek word, *aither*, that meant variously "fire" or some sort of "divine air" breathed by the gods.

F

FAIR PLAY • This California wine region is named for the town of Fair Play. According to Erwin Gudde's *California Place Names*, this town may have been named when a fight between two miners was avoided when a bystander urged fair play. Gudde also reports, however, that in 1854 there were at least eight towns across the U.S. with the same name, so perhaps something else was at play. The first citation for the phrase *fair play* was in 1595, in William Shakespeare's play *King John*.

FERMENTATION • The process of turning grape juice into wine is called *fermentation*, because it involves a lot of bubbles. The Latin word *fermentum* was carried into English by French in the 1300s but had evolved within Latin from *fervere*, meaning "to boil." As yeast consumes sugar during fermentation, it generates alcohol and carbon dioxide. The carbon dioxide bubbles up to the surface and creates a seething, boiling appearance. Also coming from the Latin *fervere* is our word *fervent*. The precursor to *fervere* was an Indo-European root, *bhreu*, also meaning "boil." This root also evolved along a separate path to produce *brew*, *broth*, and *bread*.

FIASCO • In English, we think of a *fiasco* as an "embarrassing failure," quite often one that costs money. But the word originates in Italian, where it means "bottle." The ancestor of the English word *flask* is first seen in early Latin, where it meant a small personal wine container for travel. It is thought to have been a wooden container taken along by thirsty pedestrians. Early Germanic languages also carried this word root on their journeys, so it is unclear whether Germanic got it from Latin or the other way round. Over the intervening millennia, the descendants of this word root settled in England as *flask* and in Italy as *fiasco*. It was 150 years ago that *fiasco* first showed up in English, as an expression for an embarrassing performance at the theatre. There are accounts that tell us that in both Italy and France, a disastrous theatrical performance was called *a bottle* and having one was known as *making a bottle*. Although getting into the bottle before a performance might result in a fiasco, that is not presented as a source for the expression. Instead, two theories are floated. One that has the feel of folk etymology is that glassblowers discarded flawed work and reused the material to make common bottles. The second theory, without much more evidence to support it, is that a game referred to in Italian as *make a bottle* had the loser buy the next bottle of wine.

FIDDLETOWN • This California winegrowing area takes its name from a local town. Two stories attach themselves to the name. One is that, during the time of the California gold rush, miners from Missouri came and many brought fiddles. The account says it was common to see a miner working a claim while a partner provided entertainment with his fiddle music. The second story claims that the initial settlers included a family of four violin players, who originally dubbed the place Violin City.

FIFTH • Since 1979, wine bottles in the United States have conformed to the world standard of 750 milliliters. Prior to that, the American practice had been to bottle wine in a size called a *fifth*, based on its volume of one fifth of a gallon. The reason most people don't remember wine bottles suddenly getting smaller is that a fifth was 757 milliliters, so the change amounted to a slightly less than 1 percent difference. The word *fifth*, like *five*, came to English through Old English, and through Germanic languages before that. (See **Finger Lakes**, p. 79.)

FINE • It is difficult to define what *fine wine* is, not least because the word *fine* has such an enormous breadth of meanings. Discarding those definitions that don't often apply

78

to wine, such as the *fine* that must be paid, there are *fine* meaning "superior" and *fine* meaning "delicate and subtle" in structure or texture. Both of these meanings appeared in English around 1300. Differing subtly are *fine* as an expression of admiration and *fine* meaning "elegant"— meanings that appeared after 1400. The word appears as *fino* in all of the languages that grew out of Latin, likely a common derivative of *finire*, "to finish." The idea was that something unfinished will be of lower quality and refinement than something that has been lavished with the care needed to complete its development. And yet if one were to refer in the 1500s to a *fine wine*, it might well have meant simply a wine that was clear as opposed to cloudy. *Fine*, meaning free from impurities, is still applied to gold; *fine gold* applies to 24-karat or 99.9 percent pure gold. This is also the source of the word *fining*, referring to the material used in clarifying wine.

FINGER LAKES • This winegrowing region in New York State is named for the 11 long, narrow lakes that stretch like fingers from north to south. The word *finger* came to us from Old English and its Germanic parent language. The word is shared with other languages with similar parentage, such as Danish, Dutch, German, and Swedish, but not with other Indo-European languages. The word is thought to go back to an Indo-European root, however. *Pengke* is thought to have been the Indo-European word for "five." Both *finger* and *fist* are thought to have evolved based on this root because of the hand's five fingers.

FINISH • Finish is the wine term for *aftertaste* and a long finish is a good thing. As a word, *finish* first arrived in English circa 1350 as a verb and by the later 18th century had expanded into a noun. The source was through French from the Latin *finis*, meaning "end."

FINO • Used especially with respect to sherry, *fino* literally means "fine." *Fino's* alternative with respect to sherry is *oloroso*, which means "fragrant" and is a Spanish outgrowth of the Latin *odor*, meaning "odor." (See **fine**, p. 78.)

FLAVOR • The importance of wine through the ages is attributable to the attractions of alcohol. Once the marvel of the beverage had been recognized, though, it became the work of countless generations of winemakers to produce wines of better and better flavor. That is why vines are propagated as cuttings rather than by planting seeds; once a variety has been found to display desirable attributes, growers strive to preserve these by foreclosing on the vagaries of sexual reproduction that introduce genetic diversity into seeds. While we think of flavor as happening in our mouths, we also know that when our nose is blocked our ability to appreciate flavor is diminished. The etymology of the word *flavor* coincidentally reflects this association between smell and flavor. When *flavor* appeared in English back around the year 1300, it brought with it the meaning it had held in French; that meaning was not "taste," but "aroma," "smell," or "odor." Further, the French word appeared as *flaor*, and it is suspected that the meaning of "taste" that the word acquired came along with the "v," from a conflation with the word *savor*. *The Oxford English Dictionary* cites John Milton in 1671 as the first to use the word *flavor* specifically for a sensation of taste (in another coincidence, Milton was writing about resisting wine's temptations). The etymology of the French root *flaor* is likely the Latin *flare*, meaning "blow," which unfortunately also gave English the word *flatulence*. (See **clone,** p. 53, and **taste,** p. 165.)

FORT ROSS • Fort Ross is a winegrowing area in Sonoma, California. In 1812, a settlement was founded and named *Krepost Ross* and became the center of operations for the Russian-American Company, a royally chartered trading company along the lines of England's East India Company, Hudson's Bay Company, Plymouth Company, and Massachusetts Bay Company. *Krepost Ross* translates to

"Fortress Ross," but the Ross part comes not from a personal name but from *Rossiya*, an old term that Russians used to describe themselves. To choose the name for the place, the new settlers drew lots and *Krepost Ross* was the winning entry.

FORTIFIED • Wines such as port and sherry are said to be *fortified*. This term wasn't applied to wines in English until 1906 but the root words go back to Latin and beyond. The Latin word was built on two elements, *fortis* and *fiacre*, which literally mean "strong make." The possible Indo-European root underlying *fortis* is *bherg*, meaning "high." That is appropriate both for the place where one might locate a fort and for fortified wine, which is higher in alcohol.

FOXY • Although *foxy* became a compliment for American women around 1913 (the slang term seems to have spread from Nebraska), *foxiness* in wine has been a term of severe disapproval since 1847. Native North American grapes had been called *fox grapes* since 1657, but it was only as wine drinkers accustomed to European *Vitus vinifera* flavors began to experiment with North American varieties in winemaking that the word *foxy* emerged to express an unappealing flavor element they found there. The meaning was extended to off flavors in *vinifera* wines as well. The word *fox* may have evolved from an Indo-European word meaning "animal with a prominent tail." Some scholars look at the Sanskrit word for "tail" and see a connection to a pre-Teutonic word that evolved into our word *fox* through Old English. *Fox* is the word for the male of the species and *vixen*, the word for a female fox, can mean an "attractive woman," just as *foxy* can. It makes one ponder the "tail" connection. (See **vat,** p. 174.)

FRANC • Most often encountered in the grape name *Cabernet Franc*, the designator *Franc* evolved from a parent word that ultimately applied to the Kingdom of the Franks. They were a Germanic people identified as early as the 3rd century as living in the region of modern Holland. They also gave their name to France.

FRANCE • France has been regarded by English speakers as one of the ultimate centers of fine food and wine. The country takes its name from the Franks, one of the Germanic peoples. As the Roman Empire weakened, the Franks made successful military expansions both westward and southward from what is now the northeast edge of France. Several theories exist as to how the Franks originally got their name. One suggests that their favored weapon was a javelin, whose Germanic name was *franca*. Another theory is that *franca* meant "brave" or that Franks took their name from the personal name of a leader. Yet another theory is that *frank* evolved out of *wrang*, which had a meaning of "wretched ones" or "people who have been displaced."

FRESNO • The location of the California State University (Fresno) Department of Viticulture and Enology. The name *Fresno* comes from the Spanish name for the ash tree. The species whose common name is *Oregon ash* goes by the scientific name *Fraxinus oregona*, showing that the Latin name for ash was *fraxinus*. That Latin word grew into *fresno* in Spanish.

FRIULI • The name of this region in northeastern Italy is a contraction of its name from classical times, *Forum Julii*. That meant "marketplace of Julius," referring to Julius Caesar, who regularly stationed troops in the area due to its strategic importance as a gateway into Italy between the Alps and the Adriatic. The region is also known as Friuli-Venezia Giulia. *Giulia* translates as "Julian," again referring to Julius Caesar.

FRUIT • The product of the vine is its fruit, and drinkers particularly enjoy the taste of fruit in their wines. That is appropriate to the etymology of the word *fruit*, which English got from French. Back in Latin, as *fructus*, the word underwent a change in meaning. Before meaning "the product of a vine" or other crop, *frui* had meant "to enjoy." The fact that a word associated with pleasure migrated to a group of foodstuffs shines a happy light on the lifestyle and menus of the Romans.

FUMÉ BLANC • In 1968, Robert Mondavi introduced what appeared to be a new name in wine, *Fumé Blanc*. The wine was in fact Sauvignon Blanc, but the change in name borrowed cachet from Pouilly-Fumé and, along with his other marketing innovations, proved enormously successful. But was the name so new? Near Burgundy in France, the Sauvignon Blanc vine has been known as *Fumé* or *Blanc Fumé* since 1750. *Fumé* means "smoky" and is thought to have been applied to the grapes because at maturity they appear to have a smoky film covering their skins. The French word came from Latin as *fumus*, which is believed to have evolved from an Indo-European base, *dhumo*, which co-evolved into the Sanskrit *dhumas*. Both of these words also mean "smoke."

G

GALLO • The wine giant takes its name from its founders Ernest and Julio Gallo, whose father Giuseppe (or Joe) emigrated from Italy, bringing the name that means "rooster" in Italian.

GAMAY • This grape type was named after a tiny village in France whose name was first recorded in the mid 1300s. The first citation for the grape with this name dates from 1395. It was a tempting grape to grow, due to its easy maintenance and high yield. However, it was only a few decades before higher economic interests intervened. By 1395, Philip II had long taken over the French throne from his deranged nephew Charles VI and was concerned about the economic generating power of his duchy of Burgundy. He noticed that profits from the sale of wine were down and blamed that on the widespread adoption of the Gamay grape, which, he felt, had reduced the quality of wine and, hence, the interest of buyers. His law called the Gamay a "disloyal" plant, and ordered vines to be cut down by the end of summer and uprooted by the following spring. It seems, however, that the economic decline in Burgundy was due more to the recent plague years; fewer people were buying wine because there were fewer people. The people who remained objected to the new law but Philip—also known as Philip the Bold—pressed on, jailing the Mayor of Dijon and appointing a new governor. Rather than restoring the fortunes of Burgundy, the destruction of the Gamay crop led to even more economic hardship. The pressure to produce wine with a reduced labor force meant that not all Gamay vines were destroyed. Despite centuries of being viewed as an inferior variety, Gamay survived and now thrives as the grape of the popular Beaujolais wines.

GERMANY • Julius Caesar called the Germanic peoples *Germani*, which became *Germanus* in Latin. Why Julius chose this name is a mystery, but several theories have been proposed. Celtic roots may render a meaning of "neighboring people," while a Germanic etymology might point to *gari man*, meaning "spear man."

GEWÜRZTRAMINER • If you look in a dictionary, it will likely tell you that *Gewürztraminer* is a German name for a grape type, meaning "spicy Traminer." If you look in a better-quality wine reference, it might explain that the non-German names of this grape emphasize aromatic qualities rather than spiciness. The etymology of the German *gewürz* links it to herbal fragrances, not stinging pepper. Turning within your reference to the entry for *Traminer*, you will find that the Traminer grape takes its name from a town of approximately 4000 souls in the northernmost part of Italy. It is so northernmost that, not too many decades ago, the town of Termeno (the Italian name) was part of Austria, and the townsfolk are as likely to speak German as they are Italian. That is why the grape is called by the German name of the town instead of the Italian one. It's appropriate that the town's name is rendered in languages from both sides of the border: although it's not known for certain, the name is thought to have evolved from the Latin *terminum*, meaning "border" or "frontier." *Gewürztraminer* only turned up in the English written record in 1940, while *Traminer* appeared almost 90 years earlier. These dates are partially reflective of the age of the name. *Gewürztraminer* couldn't have shown up much earlier in English because it didn't come to be applied in German until the late 1800s; in Alsace it was 1973 before it was accepted. Traminer, on the other hand, is acknowledged to be one of the most ancient grape varieties in Europe; it was known in the village that gave it its name back in the year 1000. The author who finally put *Traminer* before the eyes of English readers is worthy of note not only for this deed but also for at least one other you might recognize. Cyrus Redding wrote *A history and description of modern wines*, which was successful enough to go through four editions over 30 years, beginning in 1833. He did the hard work of his research in Paris and was the intrepid reporter who reported back to the London *Examiner,* and so to all of England, that Wellington had defeated Napoleon at the Battle of Waterloo. (See **root,** p. 147.)

GIRONDE • The river that flows through the Bordeaux region changes its name from Garonne to Gironde as it moves seaward. Both names are believed to be variations of the same word. The river was known as *Girunda* in 1253 and as *Garunda* by the Romans. One theory as to the origin of the river's name is the pre-Indo-European word *kor, kar* or *gar,* meaning "rock" and referring to the river's source in the Pyrenees. However, this etymology has been challenged, based on the thinking that the river's name would more likely be derived from its character in its wide, flat lower reaches. Alternatively, the name might have evolved from the Latin root *gyrare,* which came from the Greek *gyros,* meaning "turn," "ring," and "circle." These meanings, at least, are consistent with the nature of the river, which changes its direction of the flow with the tide.

GISBORNE • This New Zealand wine region is named after the city of Gisborne, which takes its name from a colonial secretary who was in office in 1870. William Gisborne was born in England and worked first as a respected civil servant before moving into politics, where he was evidently battered by the adversarial atmosphere. Though a fair and thoughtful man once mature, in youth Gisborne had been combative himself, having fought a duel that had somehow evolved out of some insult associated with an orange thrown during a social event.

GLASS • Having spent money on a wine, it is a shame to drink it from anything but a nice wine glass. A drinking container made of glass was, according to *The Oxford English Dictionary,* first termed *a glass* in 1392. Since then "drinking vessel" has pushed bottles, jars, and mirrors almost completely out of mind when someone imagines what is meant by the term *a glass*. The word *glass* itself arrived with the oldest of Old English, because the manufacture of glass is one of the oldest of technologies. According to John Ayto's book *Word Origins*, glass manufacture historically produced colored glass, not clear glass, and so *ghel*, the Indo-European ancestor of *glass*, was actually a color word that also gave Greek a word meaning "green" and English the word *yellow*. *The American Heritage Dictionary* assigns this same root *ghel* the meaning "to shine," and also associates this root with the word *gold*.

GOBLET • Although *goblet* today describes a drinking vessel with a stem, it originally referred to a drinking bowl without handles. It appeared in English from French in the 1300s and may have come from Celtic roots, where *gob* referred to a beak or protruding mouth. Whether this link exists is unknown, as is the extension that such a *gob* in *goblet* might refer either to a pouring spout on a bowl, or to a person's nose and mouth applied to the bowl.

GOURMET • *Gourmet* referred to the appreciation of wine before it ever referred to the appreciation of food. In Old French, a *gromet* was a "valet" and, in particular, was an assistant to a wine merchant. It took until 1820 for the expertise that these helpers picked up in the wine shop to make it into English as the word *gourmet*. Yet, for centuries before that, it had been a requirement for ships leaving port in the south of England to have a "ship's boy" on board, and these boys were referred to as *grummets*. Some sources speculate on whether this word was related to *groom*, meaning "boy" or "servant" back in Middle English. The "eating" aspect of *gourmet* may have been imposed on the word by another French word, *gourmand*, which holds a meaning not only of "one who enjoys food" but also of "glutton."

GRAFT • To protect against aphid attack, European grapevines are usually grafted onto North American rootstocks. This sense of the word *graft* comes from the Greek word for "pencil," because the shoots of vine being grafted on looked similar in size and shape. The graphite in our pencils takes its name from the same source.

GRAND • The top wines in France are referred to as *grand cru*, meaning "great growth." The word *grandis* existed in Classical Latin with a meaning of "full grown" or "big," but it was the word *magnus* that at first meant "great." Some sources indicate that the underlying meaning of the root of *grandis* was "swelling" or "enlargement," and so perhaps it's appropriate that *grandis* puffed up as *grand* and overtook *magnus* as the more prominent word meaning "great."

GRAPE • In the first half of the 6ᵗʰ century in Ireland, there lived a man named Brendan. It was the early period of Christianity in Ireland, and legend holds that Brendan and a group of monks sailed away in search of paradise—and found it. At one point along the way, the group had been adrift at sea for many days without food when God sent "a small fowl" with a "great bunch full of sweet red grapes" for them to eat. There are older sources in Latin, but the English version of this story is told in the *South English Legendary*, a document telling the tales of many saints and dating from about 1290. This represents the first time the word *grape* appeared in English. The word came to English from Old French with the Norman Conquest of 1066. It is thought that in French it had meant not just a single grape but a bunch of grapes and that the bunch took this name from the tool used to harvest them. Vines were pruned and grapes harvested with a hooked knife, and the deeper etymology for *grape* meant "hook"; that is where we get the term *grappling hook*. Before the arrival of the Old French word, Old English had used *winberi,* another word rooted in Anglo-Saxon and Germanic with the self-evident meaning of "wine berry."

GRAVES • Graves in Bordeaux is named for its gravelly soil. Evidently, a number of other French winegrowing areas were previously known by the same name, for the same reason. In Old French, smaller pebbles were not *grave* but *gravelle*, and so when William the Conqueror took over England and brought French with him, English gained *gravel* as a new word. But these French words did not come from Latin. *Gravo* was one of those Celtic words that hasn't actually been documented anywhere; instead, its existence is implied by the existence of similar words that descended into a number of Celtic languages such as Breton, Cornish, and Welsh.

GRAVES DE VAYRES • This region of Bordeaux is named for a small town located where several small streams join the Dordogne River. The root of the town's name is obscure but has been suggested to mean "water" or "green."

GREECE • The country of Greece is named for its people, the Greeks, whose name may have come from the Indo-European root *gra*, meaning "venerable."

GRENACHE • In 1851, this grape variety's name made its way into English from French, where the first citation dates from 1806. The French word came from Spanish, which in turn got it from the word *garnatxa* in Catalan, the language of the eastern region of Spain along the Mediterranean. The Medieval Catalan word is thought to have been *vernatxa* and to have been based on the Italian grape name *Vernaccia*. Unlike *Grenache*, however, *Vernaccia* has been applied to numerous grape types. Although some claims have been made that *Vernaccia* was named for the town of Vernazza in Liguria, Italy, the indiscriminate application of *Vernaccia* to many different kinds of wine and grapes during medieval times suggests instead that the name is based on the Latin *vernaculus*, meaning "native" or "indigenous." Thus, anywhere a wine trader went, the wine would be known as *vernaccia* or "locally grown." For this reason, various grapes

90

and wines in Italy are called *Vernaccia*. That simply means that each is considered native to its region and the term conveys no specific characteristics; some of the wines being red, some white, some sparkling, some still.

GRÜNER VELTLINER • The grape type Grüner Veltliner takes its name from the German word for "green" and from *Veltliner*, a designation added to several grape types thought to have originated in the valley of Valtellina in northern Italy. The valley is named for the small town of Teglio, *valtellina* translating literally as "valley of Teglio." In turn, the town's name means "lime tree." Other grape names with this designator are *Roter Veltliner*, meaning "red Veltliner"; *Frühroter Veltliner*, meaning "early red Veltliner"; and *Brauner Veltliner*, meaning "brown Veltliner."

GUENOC VALLEY • The name of this California wine area appeared first on a land grant of 1844. The word *guenoc* may have once been a Miwokan Indian word, *wenok*, meaning "medicine."

H

HANGOVER • The word *hangover* as applied to the aftereffects of alcoholic overindulgence first appeared in 1904 in a sort of a joke publication called the *Foolish Dictionary* by an author with the pen name Gideon Wurdz. Considering the fact that people have likely been suffering hangovers for many thousands of years, it is a little surprising that there seem to be so few words to describe the condition and that the ones we do have are fairly recent. The synonyms to be found in *The Oxford English Dictionary* are not much older than *hangover* and have largely fallen out of use. If you woke with a throbbing head in 1849, what you were experiencing was called a *katzenjammer*, a German word meaning "cats howling." By 1877, you might feel *chippy* the morning after. The oldest candidate dates from 1624, but *cropsick* seems to have been more related to the stomach and blamed on excessive eating as well as drinking. The paucity of *hangover* synonyms contrasts sharply with the abundance of words we use for intoxication. Perhaps that reflects human enthusiasm for discussing drinking but reticence about proclaiming any experience with the consequences.

HARVEST • You've likely heard the Latin phrase *carpe diem*, meaning "seize the day." The same Indo-European root that gave Latin *carpe* is thought to have given Germanic languages the words that in turn gave English the word *harvest*. The central idea involves plucking, grabbing, or picking, and the same root gave Greek the word *karpos*, meaning "fruit." Despite the etymology, *harvest* in Old English referred to the season, not the act. It wasn't until around 1400 that *harvest* became a verb in English.

HAWKE'S BAY • This New Zealand wine region takes its name from the bay named by Captain James Cook in 1769 after Sir Edward Hawke, First Lord of the Admiralty. Edward

Hawke had proven an extraordinarily able officer in the navy but had failed on several occasions to be elevated to political rank. The judgment of history seems to endorse this hesitancy; when he finally was promoted, he proved only an adequate administrator, whatever his earlier superiority in sea battles.

HERMAPHRODITE • Over thousands of years, vignerons have selected vines for their productivity. Early in wine history, this selection was likely done without appreciation for the fact that plants come in male and female varieties. At first, male plants would have been ripped out for their lack of fruit production. That would have severely reduced the productivity of female plants and they too would have been removed from vineyards. The few hermaphrodites—plants that accidentally inherited both male and female traits—would have fared best against these millennia of culling. The result is that domestic grape varieties are hermaphroditic while wild grapes are not. The word *hermaphrodite* is Greek and originates in the myth of Hermaphroditos. He was the son of Hermes, messenger of the Greek gods, and Aphrodite, goddess of love. Although Hermaphroditos takes his name from his two parents, his blended sexuality is supposed to have been the result of a bath in the fountain of the nymph Salmacis. She lusted after the bather to such an extent that she fused with him, thus giving him her female attributes in addition to his male characteristics.

HERMITAGE • The opulence of wines, museums, restaurants, and clubs carrying the name *Hermitage* is quite at odds with the roots of the word. In the case of Hermitage, the appellation of the northern Rhône, the name is attributed to an ancient hermit's hideaway high on the hill now known as Hermitage. Legend names the hermit as Gaspard de Sterimberg, who was also said to have brought Syrah vines to the site from the Crusades. Though this legendary source of Syrah is false, the story does underline an aspect of religious fervor that might be lost on modern drinkers of Hermitage. Since about 1800, the word *hermit* has described someone living apart from the rest of society, usually in poverty. This sense does not carry with it any reason for such antisocial behavior. Yet when *hermit* first appeared in English, around the lifetime of Gaspard de Sterimberg approximately 800 years ago, the reason for the solitude was unambiguous: dedication to God. English took the word *hermit* from French, which in turn took it from Latin. In all three languages, the leading "h" came and went with fashion. The precursor to the Latin word was without an "h," however. The Greek root was *eremos*, meaning "desolate" and "lonely," being also related to the Greek word for "desert." (See **Shiraz**, p. 156.)

HORIZONTAL • A "horizontal tasting" compares wines across the same vintage. Such wines are on the same level with respect to age and the analogy is to a flat horizon. The root of both *horizontal* and *horizon* comes from the Greek sense for geometry. An idealized horizon is flat and level all 360° around you; that is how the horizon would appear far out to sea. In such a case, the horizon is an equal distance from the viewer in all directions and forms a perfect circle. Our word *horizon* is actually an abbreviation of a Greek phrase, *horizon kyklos*, meaning "the boundary circle" from *horos*, meaning "boundary" or "limit."

HOWELL MOUNTAIN • This Napa, California, wine region is named for a mountain with a name noted back as far as the 1870s. No individual has been identified as the person who lent it that name. *Howell* is likely a Welsh family name meaning "eminent."

HUDSON RIVER • As well as being the name of the river that flows through New York City, Hudson River is also a recognized American Viticultural Area. On September 3, 1609, Henry Hudson dropped anchor in New York Bay. The river is named for his exploration, as is Hudson Bay, the gigantic subarctic gulf where he was set adrift in a rowboat to die in 1611.

HUNGARY • Wine has been produced in what is now Hungary since Roman times. The English name of the country is not what Hungarians themselves call it. They refer to it as *Magyarorszag*, meaning "Magyar land," reflecting the indigenous inhabitants, the Magyar. Although one theory as to why we call the country Hungary is that the Huns dominated this region of Europe in the 5th century, that is not always considered a legitimate etymology. Instead, the name is thought by some to have derived from *On-Ogur*, a term used to describe the confederacy of tribes of Magyar that made up Hungary in the 9th century. *On-Ogur* is said to mean "10 arrows" or "10 tribes."

HUNTER VALLEY • This Australian wine region is named after John Hunter, the second governor of New South Wales. In 1797, John Shortland was in command of a vessel seeking escaped convicts northeast of Sydney when he came upon the river that issues from this valley and named it after his superior. Shortland never did catch those convicts, who, by some accounts, captured a ship and returned to England, making the only known successful escape from the colony. Meanwhile, Governor John Hunter wasn't having nearly as good a time of it. He took over a colony where military officers were profiting through corruption, including a significant rum trade, and he was unable to bring things under control. All the while, his subordinates were undermining his authority and reputation. After five years, he was recalled to England under a cloud of criticism.

HYBRID • Dr. Richard Smart explains in *The Oxford Companion to Wine* that in viticultural terms, a hybrid is "the offspring of two varieties of different species, as distinct from a cross between two varieties of the same species of vine." He goes on to point out that the European Union prefers the term *interspecific cross* because *hybrid* "has pejorative connotations within Europe." It used to be worse. Early versions of *Encyclopaedia Britannica* began their discussion of *hybrid* by explaining: "The Latin word *hybrida*, or *hibrida*, a hybrid or mongrel, is commonly derived from a Greek word, *hubros*, an insult or outrage, with special reference to lust, hence an outrage on nature, a mongrel." The thinking was that the word *hybrid* was related to *hubris*, which originally meant "presumption toward the gods" in Greek. That turned out to be a false etymology, but it says a lot about Victorian thinking that hybridization should be seen as an insult against nature. The Romans had a more specific understanding of *hybrid*: it was the offspring of a female domestic pig (a sow), and a male wild boar. One can imagine why these genders were specified; the roving male was sneaking in for a visit. *The Merriam-Webster Unabridged Dictionary* suggests the more likely etymology of *hybrid* is that the word comes from a non-Indo-European source. The dictionary offers as a parallel *imber,* Latin for the offspring of a domestic and a wild sheep.

I & J

IMPERIAL • A wine bottle that can hold six liters—the equivalent of eight standard bottles—is sometimes referred to as an *imperial*. The implication is that the wine is worthy of an emperor or, perhaps, that the bottle itself is an emperor among bottles. The word *imperial* arose in English in 1390 from Old French and Latin. In Latin, *imperium* meant "supreme authority or power."

INOCULATE • While we think of an inoculation as a hypodermic needle injecting vaccine into our arm to protect us against disease, the etymology of the word actually takes it back to agricultural practices and the grafting of grapevines. *Oculus* was the Latin word for "eye." Just as we refer to the point where a potato sends out new sprouts as the *eye* of the potato, *oculus* was used in Latin to refer to a plant bud. So in classical times, when vines were grafted and a new bud attached, Romans used the Latin word *inoculare* to describe the process.

ITALY • The etymology of the name of this country is not universally agreed upon. English certainly got the name from the Latin *Italia*, but exactly where *Italia* originated is the question. A popular hypothesis is that it evolved from *Vitali* and applied only to the southern tip of modern Italy. Some accounts say *Vitali* was the name of a northern people who settled in southern Italy. *Vitali* is also associated with *vitulus*, Latin for "calf," by which logic southern Italy becomes "the land of cattle." Other theories attribute *Italy*'s roots to the Greek use of an Oscan name (the Osci being another ancient southern Italian people) or an Illyrian name (Illyrian languages once having been spoken in the Balkans), both of unknown meaning.

JEROBOAM • In the biblical Book of Kings, Jeroboam was a "a mighty man of valor," but in the world of wine he is a bottle that contains three liters of wine, which is the same as four standard bottles. (However, if he's in Bordeaux, he contains five liters.) This terminology may seem slightly inconsistent now, but when the word was first used in English in 1816 to describe a wine container, it referred not to a bottle but to a large bowl or goblet. Neither had its volume been pinned down by 1889, when it was reported as being a bottle big enough to contain 10 or 12 ordinary bottles.

JUG • Jug wine is inexpensive wine sold in volume. The word *jug* first appeared as a nickname for women named Jane around the time of Shakespeare. Both of the most influential English dictionaries in the world—*The Oxford English Dictionary* and *The Merriam-Webster Unabridged Dictionary*—speculate that the jug that wine comes in may be named for the women's nickname. Exactly how this use might have evolved is not explained, though an obvious guess—that women's breasts are also called *jugs*—holds no water, since this slang term didn't appear until 1957.

JURA • This eastern French wine region takes its name from the Jura mountains, which in turn are said to be named from the Gaulish word *iuri*, meaning "wooded mountain."

K

KABINETT • This German wine term designates one of several "quality wines with distinction" and is specifically tied to the levels of sugars in the grapes used. *Kabinett's* choice as an official designation is based on an older use of the term that less rigorously designated wine of high quality, particularly wine that the producers would themselves store in their own *cabinet*—a special cellar. The origin of this usage may come from one specific cellar known as the *Cabinetkeller* at the monastery of Eberbach in Germany; founded in the 12th century, it was one of the most important wine centers of the Middle Ages. The word *cabinet* is thought to have derived from the Latin *capanna*, meaning "hut"—although whether it came into German via French or Italian is disputed. *Cabinet* referred generally to a small chamber, such as the room in which special wines were stored.

KNIGHTS VALLEY • This California wine region is named for Thomas Knight, a native of Maine who stopped in the valley in 1845 and farmed it for 21 years. Some sources indicate he was forced to stop because a cask of gunpowder exploded and destroyed his entire outfit.

KOSHER • Kosher wines are wines produced only by observant Jews. In this respect, they differ from other kosher foods, for which the source of the food and the way it is processed are more important than the people producing it. The word *kosher* came into English via Yiddish and in turn from *kaser* in Hebrew. Hebrew is not an Indo-European language but a Semitic language, as is Arabic. *The American Heritage Dictionary* defines the ancient Hebrew meaning of *kaser* as "to be fitting, to succeed."

KRATER • The ancestor of our word *crater*, which describes a big hole in the ground, is a Greek word that came into Latin and was also applied to a wine mixing cup called a *krater*. Sophisticated Romans and the Greeks before them didn't drink their wine straight; instead, they watered it down. Just as some tea drinkers feel it is very important to pour the milk into the cup first, classical wine drinkers would never pour water into wine, but only wine into water. The krater was like a salad bowl in that it was used for wine preparation and then as a common serving vessel for all the drinkers. Some particularly large parties required particularly large kraters. One enormous example unearthed in 1953 in France is known as the Krater of Vix. It stands more than five feet tall and is able to hold at least 250 gallons. It had been lying buried for 2500 years.

L

LABEL • Though one should not judge a book by its cover, we all do, and the same is true for wine labels. A wine label is almost the only thing that calls to us from the shelf of a store. As important as they are, wine labels have only existed for about 150 years. Before that, it was difficult to get them to adhere to glass bottles, and even further back, wine wasn't sold in bottles. The word *label* appeared in English in the early 14th century and referred to a strip of fabric not paper. As with most words that appear in the English written record around that date, *label* came into English with the French of the Norman Conquest and had been an Old French word before that. The Old French word may have arisen from a Germanic word root, which may have given us *lap*, which in Old English meant "flap of a garment." It was the late 17th century before *label* gained the meaning it has today.

LAKE ERIE • One of the designated American Viticulture Areas is located adjacent to Lake Erie and takes its name from the lake. In 1670, as a result of his missionary travels, René Bréhant de Galinée drew a map that demonstrated that the Great Lakes were connected to one another. On this map, he documented the name *Lake Erie* for the first time. The name originates from the name of the Iroquois Erihon clan, *erihon* meaning "wildcat."

LAMBRUSCO • First seen in English documents in 1868, this name of both grape and wine comes from Italian, where *Lambrusco* literally means "grape of the wild vine." In early Latin, *labrusca* meant "wild vine" and *lambruscare* thus meant "to allow a vine to grow wild." The Latin root word *labrusca* was resuscitated for use in the scientific name *Vitis labrusca*, when a designator was needed to distinguish between the grapevines native to North America and the domesticated

European *Vitis vinifera* varieties normally used in winemaking.

LANGUEDOC • Today, Languedoc is an important wine region of France, but its name harkens back to a time when the inhabitants of southern France spoke Old Occitan. In French, the word *Languedoc* literally means "language of oc," and *oc* is also what gave Old Occitan its name. The usual translation of *oc* is "yes," and *Languedoc* thus means "language of yes." But it wasn't that the people of southern France were necessarily all agreeable that made their language notable. It was the distinct difference in their pronunciation of the word *oc* for "yes"; the people of northern France said *oïl* instead. In effect, *Languedoc* means "the place where people say *yes* so strangely, as *oc.*" Both *oc* and *oïl* evolved from the Latin word *hoc*, which meant "this." To be more precise, they evolved from an abbreviation of the phrase *hoc ille fecit*, meaning "this he did." Knowing the full phrase leads us to a better understanding of how *oc* and *oïl* could have both come from *hoc*, and also how "this" in Latin could have evolved to mean "yes" in these daughter languages. Imagine the phrase as a response to the question, "Did he do such-and-such?" Instead of saying "yes," the respondent would reply, "This he did." While the people in northern France took *hoc ille fecit* and threw away most of it, leaving *oïl* (which in present-day French is *oui*), in southern France speakers performed the same trick but retained *oc* instead. We recognize the first half of the word *Languedoc* as related to the word *language*. It too originates from Latin. In this case, *lingua* meant not only "language" but "tongue," the organ in our mouths with which we form words. As such, these words refer to something common and unchanging in human experience. Words for things with common and unchanging qualities are often particularly ancient, and both the words *lingua* and *tongue* trace back to an Indo-European word, *dnghu*, with the same meaning.

LAZIO • The Italian wine region that is rendered *Lazio* in Italian is referred to as *Latinum* in English. It is the homeland of Latin and includes Rome. Although the Romans took their name from the city, the name of their language came from the name of the larger surrounding region. The territory may have been called *Latinum* from the word *latus,* meaning "wide," perhaps because the Tiber River basin is relatively low lying.

LIBATION • If your hostess offers you a libation, chances are she is offering you an alcoholic drink of some kind. She might choose the word *libation* because she is a Classical Greek scholar, or it could just be that she is being playful and using big words. Long before a *libation* was a martini or a beer, it was an offering to the gods. English took *libation* from Latin, but Latin in turn took both the word and the concept from Greek. We shouldn't imagine Greek libations as being some high ceremonial thing, however; their libations were more closely parallel to saying grace at dinner. Before the beginning of the meal, the wine would be prepared and a first pouring would be made in honor of the gods. Sometimes, it was a more ritualized affair that included washing of hands, burning of incense, and wearing of laurel wreaths, but often a libation could be as casual as a toast mid meal.

LIEBFRAUMILCH • This name applies to a German white wine style, but initially *Liebfraumilch* referred exclusively to wine grown around Liebfrauenkirche in Worms in southwest Germany. *Liebfrauenkirche* is the name of a church that translates from German as "the church of Our Lady." A hundred years ago, *Liebfraumilch* began to be used more broadly for the easy wines that became extraordinarily popular in the latter half of the 20th century under brand names such as Blue Nun and Black Tower. One wonders whether sales would have been quite so brisk if the figurative translation of *Liebfraumilch* had been printed on the label: "Milk of the Virgin Mary."

LIGURIA • This Italian winegrowing region along the coast leading toward France is named for the Ligures, a tribal people who were one of the groups that the Romans referred to as *barbarians*. According to the *Encyclopaedia Britannica*, the Ligures lived in villages and scratched a living from the rocky soil of the mountainous region but had a reputation for toughness that made them desirable as mercenaries. (See **Barbaresco,** p. 17.)

LIMOUSIN • Oak is an important non-grape wine crop and oak from Limousin is famous for use in barrels. Perhaps people remember Limousin oak because it has a rich sound based on its association with limousine cars. Limousin oak is not especially important to winemaking, although more broadly, French oak is. Limousin oak is said to be more important to the making of brandy than the making of wine. Limousin was an area of France with the principal city of Limoges, both named because the early inhabitants called themselves *Lemovices.* The meaning of *Lemovices* is "conquering with the elm," supposedly due to the fact that the inhabitants' weapons were made of elm (not oak, ironically). These tree-named conquerors were also the source of the designation of the luxury car. These vehicles contain separate compartments for driver and passengers. Initially, the driver was not enclosed but did enjoy the protection of a cloth covering overhead. Evidently, this cloth was reminiscent of a particular kind of cloak worn by people from Limousin, and that's how the vehicle got its name.

LIQUOR • *Reflections on Ice Breaking* by Ogden Nash: Candy / Is dandy / But liquor / Is quicker. Here, the use of the word *liquor* relates specifically to distilled alcoholic beverages. The word arose from Latin and arrived in English from French along with the Normans. In Latin, *liquor*'s parent word meant something in a liquid state. That was the first sense of the word in English, when it appeared in a document known as the *Ancrene Riwle* sometime before the year 1225. This *Ancrene Riwle* might now be translated as "the Nun's Rule" and was aimed at women entering monastic life. The nuns weren't drinking whiskey because, at the time, England was unaware of the technology of distillation. It was 1250 when distillation first came to France. Thus, at first, the word *liquor* could not possibly have been applied to distilled spirits, since they weren't available. Some sources point to alcoholic beverages being termed *liquor* as early as 1300 in English, but that appears to apply only in as much as the word *drinks* might, since even in 1494 one citation read "wine, milk and other liquors." When English first adopted the word from French, it was as *licur,* but scholars recognized the word's Latin roots and imposed a more etymologically accurate "q" spelling.

LITER • In 1979, the U.S. Bureau of Alcohol, Tobacco, and Firearms required wine bottles to be sized as they were in most of the rest of the world, with 750 milliliters as the normal wine bottle volume. That is 750 thousandths of a liter or three quarters of a liter. A liter is a unit of volume adopted by France—and, subsequently, the rest of the world—after the French government in 1790 thought it might be a good idea to manage units of measurement in groups of 10; hence, the metric system. The name for units of volume was chosen to be *liter* (or *litre*) after an obsolete French unit of measure, the *litron.* The *litron* in turn had taken its name from the Latin *litra,* which before that had been a Greek word for both a unit of weight and a coin, money commonly being valued according to the weight of the precious metal used. Initially, a *liter* was defined as the volume enclosed by a cube one tenth of a meter high (and long and wide, of course; it's a cube). Conveniently, this volume appeared to enclose exactly one kilogram of water weighing 1000 grams. Isn't nature wonderful that a gram of water would fill a volume of one milliliter, which would also be one cubic centimeter? How convenient, especially since the length of a meter was chosen rather arbitrarily as one ten millionth of the distance between the North Pole and the equator. Yet by 1901, as measurement techniques evolved, it became clear that nature wasn't so wonderful after all. A kilogram of water almost, but not quite, fits into a liter.

LIVERMORE VALLEY • This California wine region is named after Robert Livermore, who arrived near Los Angeles in 1822 after a short career in England as a mason and then one on the seas as a sailor. He integrated into the Spanish community in California, marrying into a prominent family and living comfortably in both English- and Spanish-speaking spheres. He died in 1858, but he was enough of a mover and shaker that when William Mendenhall founded a city in 1869 and was looking for a name for it, he thought of Livermore, who he'd known in life. He was likely reminded of Livermore by the fact that Livermore's ranch was located nearby.

LODI • The California wine region called Lodi is named for the nearby city of Lodi, which was named in 1874, possibly after the city of Lodi in Italy. Before that, the California city was called *Mokelumne*. The fact that there are places called *Lodi* in Arkansas, Illinois, Indiana, Michigan, Minnesota, Missouri, New Jersey, New York, Ohio, Texas, Virginia, and Wisconsin didn't stop the California city from deciding this name was less confusing than *Mokelumne*. That's because there were a few other Mokelumnes in the immediate vicinity. Lodi in Italy propagated its name so broadly based on its fame as the scene of a brilliant victory by Napoleon Bonaparte in 1796. Suggestions have been made, however, that Lodi, California, took this new name because some of its residents had come from Lodi, Illinois. A popular legend was that the town was named after a locally famous racehorse, but even though a plaque explaining this origin was mounted near Lodi City Hall, the story is not considered likely.

LOIRE • The Loire Valley is named for the Loire River, which flows north and westward across France and drains approximately 20 percent of the country. The name *Loire* is adapted from the Latin *liger*, which is thought to be built on the Indo-European root *lig* or *leg*, meaning "silt," "sediment," or "mud." This root has also been linked to the word *lees*, the sediment formed in wine production. All of these words ultimately stem from *legh*, the Indo-European word for "lie" or "lay." The suffix *-er* in *liger* may represent another Indo-European root, *ar*, meaning "water."

LOMBARDY • This region of northern Italy is named for the Germanic people who occupied these lands almost 1500 years ago. They were called *Langobardus* in Latin, a name interpreted by many to mean "long beards," although some believe it meant "long axes."

M

MACERATION • This word, meaning "to soften" or "to soak," came into English from French, which got it from Latin. The root is thought to come from an Indo-European root, *mag* or *mak*, meaning to "knead," "fashion," or "fit." In the case of winemaking, maceration involves keeping grape solids in contact with liquids.

MÂCON • The name of the city at the centre of the Burgundy Mâconnais region appears on wines originating there and was seen as *Matisco* as early as the 1ˢᵗ century BCE. It is said to have evolved from a Ligurian language root meaning "forested mountains." (See **Liguria**, p. 106.)

MADEIRA • The first mention we have of Madeira in English dates from 1584, when the wines of the islands of Madeira are mentioned in a book called *The Haven of Health* by Thomas Cogan. In discussing these wines, he recommends them to old men but also includes the wise advice of that premier Roman physician, Galen: "he forbiddeth young men wine until they be five and thirtie years of age because it maketh them prone to wrath and lecherie. . ." The name of the Madeira Islands is Portuguese and was given because these islands were once a rich source of lumber, *madeira* being the Portuguese word for "wood" or "timber." This word comes from the Latin *materia*, which originally meant the inner hard wood of the tree. This inner wood got this Latin name because it was seen as the source of new growth and was thus the "mother" of the new wood, the Indo-European word *mater* meaning "mother."

MAGNUM • A magnum is a bottle containing twice the normal volume of wine. On the theory that more is better, in the mid 1700s people began calling such bottles *magnum bonum*, Latin for "great good." Rather quickly, however—

certainly by 1788—people lazily dropped the *bonum*, and we've been using the great *magnum* ever since. This is one case where the French learned something from the English about wine (and Latin), since the first citation in French for *magnum* as a double bottle occurred in 1889.

MALBEC • According to the *Dictionnaire des noms de cépages de France*, the name of this grape comes from the name of a man who helped influence its adoption. Monsieur Malbeck apparently introduced it in St-Émilion. *Malbec* as a grape name shows up as early as 1783 in French. Two other synonyms for this variety of grape are *Lutkens* (rare) and *Cot* (predominant in France). Evidently, *Lutkens* is also taken from the personal name of a promoter of this variety—in this case, a doctor from Bordeaux. The synonym *Cot* appeared simultaneously with *Malbec*, in 1783, but has a longer history. *Cot* started out as the name of the southern French town of Cahors, which in turn takes its name from the Latin name *Cadurcum*, given it by the Romans based on the tribal name of the Cadurci, a Gaulish people. *Cadurci* in turn is said to mean "boars of battle," from *catu* (meaning "battle") and *turcos* (meaning "boar").

MALMSEY • If you recognize the name of this wine, it may be because of George Plantagenet, Duke of Clarence, who was brother to King Edward IV. After some nasty sibling rivalry, he is said to have been drowned in a butt of Malmsey wine. It was all perfectly legal, mind you; his execution was authorized by Parliament. That was in 1471, less than a century after the word *Malmsey* first appeared in an English document. English wine drinkers likely got it from Dutch traders. Its ultimate source was *Monemvasia*, the name of a Greek city, though the wine was likely sourced more broadly across the Mediterranean.

MANSENG • A name applied to several types of grapes—including Petit Manseng, Gros Manseng, and Manseng Noir—

the word is seen in French documents (more specifically, Occitan documents) dating back to 1562. The origin is obscure, although the name is suspiciously similar to that of another variety, *Mancin*. This link, if there is one, doesn't help much, since *Mancin* also has an obscure etymology. One theory is that it comes from the same root as the French word *manse*, meaning a "farm" or a "manor," but this is not considered likely.

MARCHE • This Italian winegrowing region stretches along what would represent the calf of the boot shape of the Italian peninsula. *Marche* is equivalent to "marches" in English, and in both languages the meaning is "border." The area took this name because it bordered several papal states during the many centuries before the consolidation of Italy into a country in the late 1800s. The English word *march* that means "boundary" is unrelated to the one meaning "walk" or to the name of the third month of the year. Instead, like the Italian *marche*, it goes back to Latin and to Germanic before that to a root that also gave us the word *mark*. There is an etymological connection between *march*, meaning "border," and the *mark* one would make on a map. The word root also extended (as in the case of *Marche*) to refer to "territory" or "land" as well as "border," and it shows up in the name *Denmark*.

MARECHAL FOCH • The years immediately following World War I must have been a patriotic time for Alsatian grape breeder Eugene Kuhlmann. That's when he named this variety of grape after Ferdinand Foch, a marshal of France. Kuhlmann didn't stop there; he named another variety after Léon Millot, president of one of France's viticultural societies, and yet another after Lucie Kuhlmann—perhaps a figure of more personal inspiration. Ferdinand Foch was the French war hero of the day and had led the French defense against German aggression. Yet *marshal* is an honorary title, not a military rank. After the war, Foch was made a marshal of Poland as well as a British field marshal.

MARGARET RIVER • This Western Australian wine region is named after a river first noted by a European in 1831, when John Garrett Bussell made note of it in his journal. Bussell had a cousin by the name of Margaret Wyche, and it is believed that he named the river after her.

MARGAUX • This area in Bordeaux may, like Graves, be named for its soils. The French word *marne* refers to a mixture of clay and limestone, which to some degree describes the variable soils of Margaux. The *Dictionnaire étymologique des noms de lieux en France* says that the origin of the name *Margaux* is obscure but that, if it is a co-evolution of the word *marne,* it has Gaulish roots. *Le Petit Robert* points to an intermediate Vulgar Latin word, *marle,* saying that the unattested Gaulish word would have been *margila.* It may be worth touching on the meanings of *vulgar* and *unattested* in this context. Before the expansion of the Romans into much of Western Europe, the various peoples spoke in many languages and dialects. The power of the Roman Empire imposed Latin on what might be called the governments of these regions, but not on every person in every hamlet. Today, Spanish, Italian, and French are the results of the mix of those local languages with Latin. But there was a shakeout period for centuries after the collapse of the Roman Empire, when mixes of Latin and local dialects prevailed. This broad Latinate mix is called *Vulgar Latin,* and the use of the word *vulgar* here means "popular." *Margaux*'s possible root *margila* is termed *unattested* because no researcher has ever come across the word in old documents. In the case of most unattested words, researchers have come across numerous similar words that appear to be related and that imply there was likely a common root. The unattested word is what they suppose that root must have been.

MARIE JEANNE • This name for a wine bottle size of 2.25 liters or three standard bottles is unique to Bordeaux. The name is of obscure origin and it appears relatively recent. Citations before 1973 have not been identified and a 1975 document from Christie's auctioneers refers to the bottle type as rare. It is notable that the large bottle known as a *demijohn* in English has been known in French as a *dame-jeanne* since 1694.

MARLBOROUGH • This important New Zealand wine district was named in 1858 after John Churchill, the First Duke of Marlborough, whose reputation was still strong even though he'd died in 1722. His portrait in Britain's National Portrait Gallery shows angels reaching out of the clouds to touch his head. This heroic name has gone through some unexpected gyrations. It was also given to a London street upon which was situated the cigarette maker Philip Morris. The cigarette maker in turn gave this name—in the form of *Marlboro*—to a premium brand of cigarettes that was aimed first at women. When that idea flopped, American advertiser Leo Burnett hitched the brand to the manliest icon in the American psyche: the cowboy.

MARSALA • This fortified wine was famous enough that the first citation in *The Oxford English Dictionary* comes from none other than Thomas Jefferson, in 1806. The wine's source is a Sicilian town of the same name, whose etymology is Arabic, meaning "Ali's Anchorage."

MARSANNE • The name of this grape variety, first noted in French documents in 1781, was applied to the vine after the place name *Marsanne* in southeastern France. This place name in turn came from a Latin personal name, *Marcius* or *Martius*. There are numerous places in France tracing their etymology to this evidently common Roman name, which is related to *Marcus*.

MATEUS • This successful wine brand was named as part of its marketing concept in 1942 by Fernando van Zeller Guedes. A beautiful building reminiscent of a château was needed, so Guedes bought the rights to the image and name of a palace in the neighborhood of his vineyard. Mateus Palace is located in the Portuguese parish of Mateus, which is in turn named for Matthew, one of the apostles of Jesus. The name *Matthew* comes from Hebrew and means "gift of God."

MAUZAC • This variety of grape, more fully known as *Mauzac Blanc*, was first cited in French in 1564. It is suspected that the Mauzac vine is named for the French town of Mauzac in the department of Haute-Garonne, smack dab between the Atlantic and the Mediterranean, near the border with Spain. The source of the town's name is possibly a personal Latin name, *Maletius*, or a personal Gaulish name, *Mausos*.

MEAD • The word *mead* is from Old English and refers to a drink made from fermented honey. It takes its name via Germanic languages from the Indo-European root *medhu*. This same root worked its way up into Greek and became *methy*, another Greek word for "wine" in addition to the more familiar *oinos*. This parallel Greek word *methy* comes through to English in *methanol*, as well as *amethyst*, a gemstone ancients believed prevented drunkenness. (See **amethyst**, p. 8.)

MÉDOC • The origin of the name *Médoc* is easy to find, but not in authoritative sources. Many resources say the Latin name for the area, *Pagus Medulorum*, meant "middle country" and referred to Médoc's position between the Gironde estuary and the Atlantic Ocean. The implication is that *Médoc* comes from *Medulorum*, which in turn came from the Latin *medius*, meaning "middle." However, many of these same sources include mention of the Medulli, a people named by the Romans as occupying the area. It isn't completely clear that *Medulorum* didn't evolve out of *Medulli* instead of *medius.*

MELCHIOR • A Melchior is a bottle large enough to contain 24 standard bottles of wine. The name comes from one of the three wise men, who was called *malki-or* in Hebrew and whose name means "my king of light."

MELCHIZEDEK • This name for an enormous wine bottle is taken from the biblical name of a king of Salem (*Salem* itself being a contraction of *Jerusalem*), whose name in Hebrew breaks down to *melek* (meaning "king") and *sedeq* (meaning "righteousness"). The volume of a Melchizedek bottle is 30 liters or the equivalent of 40 standard bottles.

MELON • The word *melon* represents both the name of a grape type and a tasting term. It's included along with other fruits like pineapple and banana on the aroma wheel, a wine-tasting tool. Each of these two *melons* has its own etymology. The grape type that produces Muscadet may owe its name to a metaphor for sweetness. The French word for "honey" is *miel,* from the Latin *mel,* and this word may have morphed to *melon.* Another theory is that the grape was named after a now-obscure fruit called a *medlar,* or *mespilum* in Latin. It has the appearance of a small brown apple and is an unlikely etymological source for *melon,* although it does have the merit of having been called an *open arse* in Old English, based on the cavity between the lobes on the end of the fruit which had once formed the flower. Evidently, this view of the fruit was not uncommon, because the Norman French called the thing *cul de chien*—colloquially, "dog's ass." Other theories for the origin of *melon* as the name of a grape relate to the shape of the vine's leaves, the shape of the grape seeds, or the mixed heritage of the vine reflected in the Latin word for "mix," *misculare.* Of course, the possibility that the grape is actually named after the gourd called a *melon* cannot be ignored. If this was the case, the parallels could be the grape's musky scent and flavor, as well as its amber-toned color. If the grape name/gourd name etymology was valid, we could follow *melon* back through Latin into Greek. *Melon* didn't originally mean "gourd" at all. What the ancient Greeks thought of as a *melon* was what we would call an *apple*. To them, adding the word *pepon* (meaning "ripe") to the word *melon* (meaning "apple") created a word that meant "melon." *Melopepon* entered Latin, but the Romans then dropped the *pepon* ending, so that by the time *melon* got into French in the 13th century, it had taken on our meaning. (See **Muscadet**, p. 123.)

MENDOCINO • Mendocino County in California and the winegrowing area therein take their name from a Cape Mendocino that began appearing on maps in 1587 as *Cabo Mendocino*. The location of this cape drifted around for a while, and the reason it was called *Mendocino* has never been definitively explained. But there are at least three theories. The first is based on a claim made in the early 1600s that, in the 1540s, two ships returning from the Philippines made landfall in this area and named the place after Don Antonio de Mendoza, the then-viceroy of New Spain. A second theory is that it was named during the 1580s after another viceroy, Lorenzo Suarez de Mendoza. Either of these claims rests on the adoption of the viceroy's last name, which was not the Spaniards' normal practice for naming geographical features. For this reason, the third theory is that a European mapmaker appended the name to a map for reasons unknown and without any real connection to the place being labeled.

MERITAGE • In 1988, some California winemakers publicized a contest through *The Los Angeles Times*. The objective was to choose and generate publicity for a new name to be applied to blended wines made in America in the style of Bordeaux. Neil Edgar won the contest when he suggested *Meritage* as a portmanteau of *American montage*. However, the group that gave him the prize liked it not because of *American montage*, but because they could imagine within it

118

merit and *heritage*. They wanted to present their wines as having merit, but they also wanted some of the gloss of Bordeaux heritage. Edgar's prize was two bottles of each of the first 10 years of Meritage wine produced by members of the newly minted Meritage Association.

MERLOT • The name of this important variety means "little blackbird." In Classical Latin, a blackbird was called a *merula*. This bird word didn't show up in the French written record until 1165, when it appeared as *merle*. By 1483, *merle* had become an English word too, also meaning "blackbird." There are two theories as to why the grape might have been named after a blackbird. The more likely seems to be the dark color of both grape and bird. An alternative may be a particular enthusiasm for the grapes by these (under the circumstances) unwelcome birds. It was 1783 before the name appeared in a French document as *merlau* in relation to the vine. It first showed up in English as *murleau*, in 1825.

METHUSELAH • This is a designation for a bottle big enough to hold as much as eight standard bottles or six liters. According to the biblical Book of Genesis, Methuselah was a patriarch and grandfather to Noah, who built the ark. Methuselah is claimed to have lived to be 969. From Hebrew, this name has been interpreted as meaning "man of the javelin," "man of Selah," or "man of Lach." *Selah* and *Lach* are understood to be the names of the deity.

MISSION • The word *mission* has a long history in the world of wine, based on the Franciscan missionaries who planted vineyards in Mexico and what is now California. English got the word from French but its roots are in the Classical Latin *mittere*, meaning "let go" or "send." The root comes through in other words in English, including the name of the religious observance called *mass*, which is a sending of thanks.

MOËT & CHANDON • In 1743, Claude Moët founded the company that still bears his name. But his name had been changed from LeClerc back in 1429. Charles VII had for years struggled to legitimize his claim to the throne of France. As he finally proceeded into Reims Cathedral to be crowned, LeClerc, one of his soldiers, shouted from the sidelines *het moet zoo zijn*, Dutch for "it must be so." The King declared that LeClerc henceforth be known as Moët.

MOLISE • According to *The Concise Dictionary of World Place-Names*, this Italian wine region may take its name from a Latin word, *mola,* meaning "mill," or derive from a nobleman from Moulins-la-Marche in France. How might a French nobleman have given his title to an Italian region? One suggestion is that along with the Germanic Lombards who pressed into Italy after the collapse of the Roman Empire came Normans. One problem with this theory is that Lombardy is in the north of Italy and the invaders would have been coming from the north, while Molise is two thirds of the way down the Italian peninsula. Another problem is that Lombardy is a rich territory but Molise even today is a poor, lightly populated, mountainous region—so of reduced appeal to Norman invaders. Even if the Moulins-la-Marche source is true, the connection between the name *Molise* and the Latin word *mola* would remain: the word *moulin* itself means "mill" and evolved from the Latin.

MONDEUSE • This is the name of a grape type, for which two etymologies have been suggested. The more likely is that *Mondeuse* grew out of the French word *monder*, meaning to "trim" or "prune," from the Latin word *mundare*, meaning "to clean." The notion is that this variety of vine sheds its own leaves around harvest time. The alternative is that *Mondeuse* is related to the Latin *mustum*, suggesting that these grapes produce particularly high quantities of juice or "must."

MONTEREY • The name of Monterey County in California was first applied to the bay that lies between the cities of Monterey and Santa Cruz. The first Spanish explorer who "discovered" it named it "bay of pines." A second Spanish explorer renamed it after St. Peter, then in 1602 Sebastián Vizcaíno dropped anchor and re-renamed the bay after Gaspar de Zúñiga y Acevedo, the viceroy for New Spain. It wasn't his title as viceroy that was applied to the bay, however; it was his title as Count of Monterrey, Monterrey being the location of his castle back in Spain. The word *monterrey* means "mountain of the king."

MOSEL or MOSELLE • These are the German and French names for the river that gives its name to this wine region. The name is a diminutive and literally means "little Meuse," the Meuse being a longer river to the west and north. The name of the Meuse derives from a Germanic word, *mos,* meaning "marsh", which also gave English the word *moss.*

MOURVÈDRE • This grape variety of Spanish origin has a name derived from a city that has since been re-named. Just north of the city of Valencia on the Mediterranean coast is the town of Sagunto, once known as *Mervidro,* the source of the name applied to this vine. The *Mervidro* name was based on the city's antiquity. About 2500 years ago, it was a walled town. During the latter part of the time when Latin was being used in this region, these walls were already old. The name *Mervidro* is said to have come from the Latin *muri veteres,* meaning "old walls."

MOUSSEUX • The French word for sparkling wine first appeared in English via the pen of travel writer Philippe Thicknesse in 1777. In his account of travels through France, he touched on the practice of tailoring wines for their intended market, saying that Champagne back in England is better than what can be had in Champagne itself, because the local stuff is not as sweet. He displays ignorance, however,

121

when he reports that the only difference between still wine from Champagne and "that which is mousser" is the time of the year in which it was bottled. Thicknesse appears to have been pretty difficult to get along with; his biography is a seemingly nonstop list of disagreements with others. His son George was so aggrieved that he felt the need to change his name from Thicknesse to Touchet. Thicknesse then expressed his regret at being George's father—as part of the subtitle to a book, no less. In bringing *mousseux* to English, Thicknesse brought a French word for "foam" and "bubbles" that was related to other words already in English. *Mousseux* came to French from a Germanic root meaning "marsh" or "wet place" that also gave English the word *moss.*

MOUTON CADET • This famous Bordeaux brand takes its name from two attributes of the wealthy and famous Rothschild family that owns it. The word *mouton* is related to the English word *mutton,* both deriving from the Latin *multo,* meaning "ram" or "sheep." But unlike the California wine region Carneros, Mouton Cadet is not associated with sheep based on past grazing areas. Instead, *mouton* specifically means "ram" as a symbol of strength, based on the fact that in medieval France *mouton* meant "battering ram" or a kind of catapult. Fittingly for such an affluent family, the word *mouton* during the 13th century also referred to a denomination of gold coin. The word *cadet* is applied to the wine because of its originator. We think of a cadet as a student in military training. However, when *cadet* first entered English from French in 1610, it meant "the youngest son in a family," which was the position of Baron Philippe de Rothschild. The word arose from a Latin word, *caput,* meaning "head," from an Indo-European *kaput* with the same meaning. Yet by the time it appeared as *cadet,* it had undergone an extension into *capitellus,* meaning "little head"—as befits the junior sibling—before its contraction to *cadet.* The military meaning arose because it was customary for prominent families to send their younger sons to attend the French royal court and train as officers.

MÜLLER-THURGAU • In 1882, Hermann Müller was working in Germany to improve the ripening date of vines that might give fruit similar to Riesling. The product of his efforts was named not only after him but also after his home canton of Thurgau in Switzerland. The English equivalent of Müller is Miller, with the self-evident etymology relating to a family history related to milling. Thurgau takes its name from the Thur River plus *gau*, meaning "district" in German. The Thur River is named based on the Indo-European word *dur*, meaning "current."

MUSCADELLE, MUSCADET, and MUSCAT • Although these names and others (Moscatel, Moscato, Muscadel, Muscatel) apply to more than one kind of grape, to wines made with yet other grapes, and even to winegrowing regions, all these words point back to the same etymological root: *musk*. It is the especially aromatic nature of some of the associated grapes that is at the root of the names. Authorities have suggested that one or another of these grape types was what the Roman botanist Pliny called *uva apiana*, "the grape of the bees," and that the reason bees liked it so much was its strong scent. This idea has led further, to the suggestion that the words' roots evolved from the Latin word *musca*, meaning "flies," which also followed the scent. Yet all the etymological big guns point to the Latin *muscatus*, meaning "having the flavor of musk." Grapes were not the only fruit to be so called; pears too were cited as *muscatelles*. In turn, the Latin word *muscus* came from the Greek *moskhos*, and both are related to near-identical words in numerous Indo-European languages. Most fascinatingly, the Sanskrit *muska* means "scrotum" and "testicle," based evidently on a visual similarity to the musk sac of certain animals. (Although the aromatic/pheromone connection between musk and sex cannot be ignored.) The *American Heritage Dictionary* goes so far as to propose that these words may have evolved from the Indo-European root word *mus*, meaning "mouse." This theory is based on how a testicle moves beneath the skin and is a parallel with the etymology of the word *muscle*. In both cases the movement was thought to be analogous to a mouse moving beneath a skin or blanket.

MUST • The mix of crushed grapes and grape juice that has yet to become wine is called *must*. English got this word directly from Latin as one of the words Old English adopted from the Latin of the Christian Church, before all the Latinate words arrived with the French of the Norman Conquest. The Latin parent word, *mustum*, was probably an abbreviation of *mustum vinum*, *mustus* meant "new," so the product of the grape crushing was thus being called "new wine."

MUSTARD • Although *mustard* may not seem to be a word related to wine, it is. Dijon mustard is commonly made with wine, and in some measure this process continues a tradition stretching back to Roman times and links the foodstuff to its etymology. The Romans often mixed their powdered mustard seed with young wine. The result was a fairly spicy condiment and *ardens*, the Latin word for "burning," was applied to the mix. In Latin, young wine was called *mustum*, thus, our word *mustard* translates as "burning wine."

N

NAPA • The Napa Valley is famous for its wine, but it isn't completely clear why it's called *Napa*. All sources point to a Native American Indian word, but just what that word meant can't be nailed down. Some claim the Patwin people called the grizzly bear *napa*. A related group of people known as the Suisun are said to have used *napa* to mean "near mother" or "near home," while to still another group it was supposed to have meant "house." *Napa* is used as a place name as early as 1795, in baptismal records. It is first cited as an Indian word in 1823, when a diary entry claims the place is named after the Indians who once lived there.

NEBBIOLO • This grape type was mentioned first in English by Thomas Jefferson, writing in 1788. Its first use in Italy dates back much earlier, to 1303. The name has been suggested to be related to the Latin *nobile*, meaning "noble," but most etymological observers think it more likely evolved from *nebula*, meaning "mist," "fog," or "cloud." This *nebula* is the same word first used by Edmond Halley in 1718 to refer to the cloudy look of some features of the night sky. Before Latin, the word was known in Greek as *nephos* and Indo-European as *nebh*, both meaning "cloud." As applied to the Nebbiolo grape, if the etymology is correct, this cloudiness may refer to the white dusting on the skin of the fruit or to the fogs that often envelop the Piedmont region of Italy during harvest. (See **bloom**, p. 23.)

NEBUCHADNEZZAR • The Babylonian ruler who lived from 604 to 562 BCE gave his name to a bottle large enough to contain 20 standard bottles' worth of wine. This use turned up first in 1907 for Champagne and had made it into English by 1913.

NEGOCIANT • The French word for a wine merchant, *negociant* only came into the English written record in 1910 but entered French from Italian in 1550. A negociant doesn't just sell wine, nor simply negotiate in its trade, but takes an active hand in buying grapes or must, or in blending finished wine and bottling and labeling it. This full involvement is real work, so the roots of the term *negociant* are actually applicable. Like the English word *negotiate*, this French term comes from the Classical Latin word *negotiari*, meaning not only "business" and "work" but also "difficulty" and "trouble." The Latin breaks into two parts, *neg* and *otium*, and since *otium* meant "leisure" and "ease," it's self-evident that *negotiari* figuratively meant "not easy."

NEGRETTE • This French grape variety is named for its dark color. This name self-evidently comes from the same roots as "the N word," *nigger*, now said by some to be the most obscene word in the English language. The Latin root that gave us both words was *niger*, which simply meant "black." The Latin word in turn comes from the Indo-European word for "night," *nekw* or *negw*. *Night*, by the way, comes from the same source via Old English and, thus, Germanic routes.

NEW ZEALAND • It isn't the sea that surrounds New Zealand that gave it its name; it was the Dutch in 1643. As the first European discoverers of these islands they named them New Zealand after the province of Zeeland in Holland.

NIAGARA • One of the main winegrowing areas in Canada. Niagara takes its name from the Mohawk words *ohnya kara*, meaning "neck of land" and designating the relatively narrow portion of land that separates lakes Ontario and Erie.

NOBLE • In English as in French, *noble* holds a meaning of "distinguished," " magnificent," or "high ranking," and in the world of wine it is sometimes applied to the most respected grape varieties, such as Cabernet Sauvignon, Pinot Noir,

Chardonnay, Riesling, and others. It is also applied as *noble rot* to botrytis, the fungus that produces Sauternes. This distinguished sense comes from Latin, where *nobilis* meant "well known" and referred to people from high-ranking families. This Latin word had earlier been *gnobilis* and arose from an Indo-European root, *gno*, which also gave English *know*.

NORTON • This is an unusual grape type for wine in that it is a native American variety and so not *vinifera*. It is named for Daniel Norborne Norton, the Richmond, Virginia, doctor who in 1822 turned to farming and grape growing as a distraction from his grief at the loss of his young wife and child.

NOSE • Because our sense of taste is strongly influenced and complemented by our sense of smell, our noses give us a lot to be thankful for in tasting wine. Not only do we use our noses in exploring a wine's bouquet, but we have also applied the word *nose* to the aromatic qualities of wine and to the action of evaluating those smells. The word describing the protruding part of our faces has been a part of English as long as there has been English. The word first appears in works by some of the earliest writers of Old English and is easily traced back to the Germanic parent languages that evolved into Old English. Words that refer to a widely common thing or experience, especially words that regularly come up in conversation, tend to remain fairly stable in form and meaning over long periods of time. Because many people know the word, it's more likely that someone will catch you if you pronounce it incorrectly or use it in an unconventional way. Since the nose is a prominent part of our bodies—certainly a noticeable part—it's no surprise that the word *nose* can be traced back past its Germanic roots and solidly into Indo-European. But language is also built by analogy. Speakers try to enliven their discourse by using well-known words in new but parallel applications. For example, before text messaging, *chat* was restricted to audible communication. As long as new analogies seem attractive to other users, words can be used in extended senses (otherwise, innovators get "corrected"). Thus, toward the end of the 1800s, the noun *nose* took on new meanings. At first, it meant the smell of barns and hay; by 1936, one might evaluate the nose of a wine. The verb *to nose* is also a latecomer as concerns sniffing a glass of wine. The verb evolved out of the noun around 500 years ago, but it wasn't until the 1960s that drinkers were said to nose their wine.

NOUVEAU and NOUVELLE • In the world of wine, *nouveau* refers to a style of wine intended for immediate consumption, while *Nouvelle* is the name of a grape type. Both words come from the French word for "new," which in turn arose from Latin but more anciently from the Indo-European word *newo*.

O

OAK • The first mention of the word *oak* in English is in a document known as *Bald's Leechbook*, thought to date from the 9ᵗʰ century. That makes *oak* a word with Old English origins and, as such, of Germanic language stock. Other Germanic languages have related words for oak, but connections to the Latin word *aesculus* and Greek word *aigilops* (both designating a particular species of oak) are speculative. In winemaking, oak is valued for the complementary flavor elements it can contribute to wine, and European oak is preferred to American oak as being subtler and less astringent. Astringency, though, is one of the reasons that oak is mentioned in *Bald's Leechbook*. A leechbook was a medical text, and it was the astringent or puckering qualities of oak bark that were being called for to quicken healing.

OAK KNOLL • This California winegrowing region was named after the estate of Joseph Warren Osborne, who purchased land in 1851 and developed it sufficiently that in 1856 it was named the best farm in California by the State Agricultural Society. Osborne met a sticky end in 1863, when a former employee named Charles Brittian shot him in an argument over a bounced paycheck.

ORGANIC • The relatively recent emphasis on organic food and wine is predated by a long history of the word *organic* that includes a surprising diversity of meanings. It was 1942 when *organic farming* got its first mention and 1960 before we saw the first citation for *organic food*. Roughly between 200 and 400 years ago, something that was organic was related to a musical instrument—not always a pipe organ, but often a wind instrument. It was the "instrumental" nature of musical instruments—that is, their nature as tools—that allowed them to be called *organs*, because the ancient Greek *organon* and then the Latin *organum* meant "tool." Tools usually have a specific function, and it is the importance of the functions of hearts, livers, lungs, and so on that resulted in their being referred to as *bodily organs*. It was also this importance of function that resulted in the first citation for the word *organic* in English, sometime before the year 1400, with a meaning of "jugular vein." If an organ is an important part, then something that is organized is something that has all the needed important parts. It was this sense of coming from a whole—something with all the parts needed to live—that lent *organic* its meaning of "a natural growth." The root of that ancient Greek word *organon* was the Indo-European *worg* or *werg*, meaning "to do," which was also the ancestor to our English word *work*.

ORVIETO • These wines are named for the Italian town near which they are produced. The town's name comes from the contraction of the Latin name *Urbs Vetus*, meaning "old town"; there had been a settlement there since Etruscan times.

OXIDATION • Wine or even must exposed for too long or to too great a degree of oxygen undergoes oxidation. This process is clearly named for the oxygen that does the damage. But the name of the element that we need to breathe in order to live takes its name from acid. During the late 1700s, when chemistry was not quite as sophisticated as it is today, it was thought that acid was produced from oxygen. Acid was metaphorically thought to have a sharpness to it, and so the stuff that created it takes its name from the Greek for "sharp maker." In Greek, *oxy* meant "sharp" and the suffix *gen* meant "make," as seen in the English word *generate*.

P

PALATE • Someone with a sophisticated palate is able to pick out more nuances when tasting wine. This sense of the word *palate* refers to a person's taste and sense of taste, even though the part of the mouth called the *palate* contains no taste buds. *Palate* refers to the roof of the mouth and is used in an extended sense to mean "taste" in the same way that *tongue* is used to mean "language." The association between *palate* and taste was made long before the word arrived in English. The English word was adopted from French after the Norman Conquest, but the Latin parent word *palatum* had already conveyed these dual meanings. The reasons that Latin adopted the word in the first place are not certain, but several dictionaries suggest a possible root in the Etruscan word *falandum*, meaning "sky," the analogy being to an over-arching structure. Although the transference in meaning from "the roof of the mouth" to "taste" occurred thousands of years ago, *The Oxford English Dictionary* indicates that it was only in 1973 when *palate* was used as a flavor attribute for wine or beer. That is to say that Roman senators may have had refined palates long ago, but no wine had a fruity palate until the last half century.

PARIS • The capital city of France is a longstanding center of the world wine trade. The name *Paris* was taken from the Latin name *Civitas Parisiorum*, meaning the "City of Parisii," the Parisii being a Celtic tribe that occupied the region. Several unlikely etymologies for this tribal name have been proposed, including the Latin *Bar Isis*, meaning "son of Isis"; the Greek *Baris*, meaning "boat'" and Celtic *par gwys*, meaning "boat men." Adrian Room, in his book *Placenames of the World*, instead suggests that the Parisii named themselves for a Celtic god and laments the durability of the "boat" theories propagated in part on the city's coat of arms.

PASTEURIZATION • At the grocery store, the dairy section is stocked with pasteurized products. These have undergone a quick heating and cooling process designed to kill pathogens that might otherwise kill grocery store customers. The process is named after Louis Pasteur, the famous French scientist who invented it. Yet for all the illness and death that pasteurization has prevented, Louis Pasteur wasn't aiming at dairy products when he invented pasteurization; he was aiming at keeping wine from becoming vinegar. It was an effort to protect the economic interests of the wine industry. Pasteur had first proved that fermentation didn't occur by magic but by living things we now call *yeast*. Expanding on the idea that it was itty-bitty creatures that turned grapes into wine, Pasteur thought perhaps there were itty-bitty creatures that turned wine into vinegar. Logically, if the creatures could be killed, the wine could be saved. These days, pasteurization is very popular for dairy products but not at all popular for the better classes of wine, which can be protected in other, less damaging ways.

PASO ROBLES • The California region originally named *El Paso de Robles* was named for its oak trees. *Robles* is Spanish for "oak trees" and evolved from the Latin *robur*, a word that denoted a particular kind of oak tree. The source of the Latin word was an Indo-European word *reudh* meaning "red" that was applied because of the color of the wood of this species of oak. Based on the strength of oak trees the Latin *robur* also came to mean "strength" and is the root of the English word *robust*. *Paso* is analogous to the English word *pass* and both words originate in the Classical Latin word *passus*, meaning "step," which is also where *pace* comes from. *Passus* in turn came from the Latin *pandere*, meaning "to stretch," and this etymology brings an unexpected connection with wine. In the 15th and 16th centuries, *pass* was also an English word meaning "raisin wine," after a Latin word, *passum*, with the same meaning. Whereas *pandere* was applied to stretching one's legs, the wine was named for "spreading out" the grapes to dry.

PAUILLAC • The place name *Pauillac* is seen as early as the 4th century as *Pauliacus* and is believed to derive from a Latin personal name, *Paulius*. In medieval usage, names derived from the Latin *Paulus* were given names, but in classical times it was a family name and originally meant "small." The first citation for Pauillac in English was in 1858 in an American business guide entitled *A Cyclopedia of Commerce and Commercial Navigation*. The primary focus of the *Cyclopedia* was North American, which may explain why, in mentioning Pauillac, it took no notice of the French classification of growths that had been established just three years before. When the *Cyclopedia* says, "third-rate wines comprise those called Pauillac, Margaux, St. Jullien, St. Estèphe, St. Emilion," it contrasts sharply with the 1855 French classification that awards premier cru status to three Pauillac wines.

PÉTILLANT • A French word that has described sparkling eyes since 1480, then a sparkle in wine since 1660, *pétillant* had been adopted into English with the same meaning by 1783. *Pétillant* denotes a very slight degree of effervescence. Unfortunately, the root of the word is not quite so delicious. The French root is *pet*, dating to 1179, from a Latin root *pedere*, meaning "to fart." It is noted in *The Oxford English Dictionary* as having an Indo-European root that was onomatopoeic—which is to say, a word that got its sound from the thing it was attempting to describe.

PETITE or PETIT • This French adjective means "small" and is often added to grape names to designate a different but supposedly similar variety in smaller form. Examples include *Petite Sirah* and *Petit Verdot*. This French word did not grow out of Latin, per se, but appeared around the 10th century as a Gallo-Roman word at first meaning "youthful" or "not fully grown." It's easy to see how a word meaning "not fully grown" could shift to mean "small."

PFALZ • The name of this German winegrowing area harkens back to the Latin it comes from. The city of Rome is built around seven hills. The central one is called *Palatine Hill* or, in Latin, *Palatium.* That is where the Roman emperors built their houses and, over time, a grand house began to be referred to as if it belonged on the *Palatium.* This is not only the ultimate root of *Pfalz* but also of our English word *palace.* But it was a system of political rule that gave the Pfalz region its name, not any grand palace located there. Areas that were governed by powerful rulers began to be called *palatine;* it was as if their rulers too belonged on the Palatine Hill in Rome.

PHYLLOXERA • Phylloxera is the Greek name of an American bug. These aphids were in all probability what kept early American settlers from being successful in establishing a wine industry in eastern North America; the European vines they planted did not survive. In the 1800s, Europeans began experimenting with North American grape varieties and unwittingly imported phylloxera aphids along with the vines. The result nearly ended European winemaking, which was particularly significant because France, Italy, and Spain alone produce almost half the world's wine. The aphids damage the roots of vines as they feed on them; under aphid attack, roots become unable to supply the remainder of the plant with nutrients or water, and the leaves dry up. Hence the word *phylloxera* is formed on two Greek elements: *phyllo*, meaning "leaf," and *xeros*, meaning "dry." We can also hear these etymologies in other, more familiar words, such as *foliage* and the corporate name Xerox, taken because its photo-reprographic process was a dry process. (See **aphid**, p. 10.)

PICCOLO • A word that means "small" in Italian, *piccolo* makes several appearances in the world of wine. A waiter's assistant is sometimes referred to as a *piccolo* and a wine bottle containing one quarter of a standard sized bottle is also sometimes called a *piccolo.* A smaller variety of Sangiovese grape is called *Piccolo,* and an Italian sweet wine grape takes its name, *Picolit*, from the small quantities of berries produced.

PIEMONTE • Piemonte or Piedmont, in the northwest corner of Italy, is surrounded both to its north and west by the Alps. This geography gives Piemonte its name, since from the Latin *pedis* and *montis*, *Piemonte* literally means "foot of the mountains."

PINOT or **PINEAU** • Both variations of this word have a particularly old provenance, dating in French to the 12ᵗʰ century. It took one of the early French-English dictionary writers, Randal Cotgrove, to bring it to English in the form of *pynos* in 1611. Etymological dictionaries are unanimous in attributing this grape name to the grape cluster's similarity in shape to a pinecone. Since pinecones themselves come in various shapes, part of the analogy might be that the tightness of the grape cluster resembles the overlapping scales of a pinecone. The word *pine* goes back much further than *Pinot*, through the Latin *pinus* and Greek *pitys*. Its roots may lie in an Indo-European base, *pica*, which didn't mean "pine" but instead meant "to swell" or "fat." The thinking here is that pine resin was likened to fat. This same root shows up in Sanskrit as *pitu*, meaning "food" or "drink," as well as in the Sanskrit word *pitudaru*, denoting a kind of pine tree.

PINOT GRIGIO and GRIS • *Grigio* and *gris* are Italian and French, respectively, for the color gray—a color whose name traces back to Indo-European and emerged as a very common color word in many of Indo-European's daughter languages.

PINOT NOIR • *Noir* is the French word for "black" and is often applied to dark grapes. It links etymologically back to the Latin word *niger*, meaning "black," and comes out of the shadows in English in the words *denigrate* and, offensively, *nigger*. (See **Negrette**, p. 126.)

PINOTAGE • This grape variety was created in 1924 from Pinot Noir and the grape known then in South Africa as Hermitage (Cinsaut). It was named by blending those grapes' names.

PIQUETTE • Wine is a prestige product that has always been too expensive for regular consumption by the poorer segments of any society. In France in the 1500s, the word *piquette* appeared to describe the stuff the laborers were given to drink instead. Considerably cheaper because it was produced by adding water to the already-used waste solids from wine production, piquette had a small percentage of alcohol to ward off waterborne disease but not much else to recommend it. Just as wine turns to vinegar, the drink took on a sour taste that pricked at the taste buds and so acquired its name *piquette*, meaning "little picker" or "little pricker."

PLONK • In 1914, World War I broke out and by 1915, Australia had joined the fighting. By 1916, all Australian forces were transferring to France, and it is thought that this is where the word *plonk* was created. *Plonk* means "cheap wine," but it's likely that *plonk* is a humorous modification of *blanc* for "white wine." From the same theatre of battle seems to have come *von Blink*, also meaning *vin blanc* or "white wine" but mispronounced to sound as if it were a name of the German enemy. Though *plonk* as wine—red or white—didn't appear in the written record until 1933, 15 years after hostilities had ended, in 1930 *plinkity plonk* appears with the same meaning, perhaps as an intermediary stage before *plonk* took hold as the favored term.

POLLEN • Pollen is the means by which flowers are fertilized in order to produce fruit. *Pollen* is a word that has been around since ancient Roman times, but it wasn't applied to a component of the vegetable sex act until 250 years ago. Before that, *pollen* simply meant "powder" or "flour." The word root is thought to extend back to Indo-European and relate to the Latin *pulvis*, meaning "dust," which gave English *pulverize*.

POMEROL • *Pomerol*, the name of the Bordeaux wine region, is one of dozens of place names that evolved from the Latin word for "orchard," *pommarium. Pomme* is French for "apple."

PORT • The fortified wine called *port* takes its name from the name of the city it was shipped from, *Oporto*, known in Portuguese as *Porto*. The entire country of Portugal takes its name from the city. But the city's name itself is an abbreviation. It had been *Portus Cale* in Latin, meaning the "port of Cale" after the earlier name of a settlement at the mouth of the Douro River. The Latin word *portus* itself originated from an Indo-European root, *per*, meaning "to pass over." How that came to mean "harbor" in Latin is somewhat illuminated by another word that arose from the same root: *ford*. A ford is a shallow place where one can safely cross a river, and *port* has an analogous meaning as being a passage—perhaps shallow—into which ships might enter and be protected from the dangers of the open sea.

POUR • The word we use to describe the transferring of wine from one container to another appeared in English documents about the right time to have been adopted from the French that arrived with William the Conqueror. If indeed *pour* came from French, its parent word was *purer*. However, its meaning must have been in flux at the time, because the earlier French meaning was closer to "squeeze," as in "to extract juice" from fruit. French documents containing *purer*, meaning "decant," only appear after the first citations for *pour* in English. The "squeeze" meaning of *purer* actually reflects a sense of separation of what is wanted (the juice) from what is not. *Purer* evolved from the Latin *purare*, meaning "to purify," and goes further back to an Indo-European root, *peu*, meaning "to purify" or "to cleanse." The first citation for *pour* in *The Oxford English Dictionary* circa 1330 does indeed concern the pouring of wine. For most of its history, wine was not the unclouded liquid we expect today, and it is consistent with this etymology that pouring could relate to the separation of wine from sediment and impurities.

PREMIER CRU • The top rank of wines are called *premier cru* or *premier cru classé*. The idea of being first is a concept that goes back a long way. It is a fundamental enough idea that both French and English gained a form of the word *prime* independently from Latin before the Norman Conquest of 1066. The Latin root *prismo* is traced back to an Indo-European root, *pro*, meaning "before" or "in front."

PREMIÈRES CÔTES DE BLAYE • Blaye is a city in Bordeaux. The *Société des Amis du Vieux Blaye* (Society of Friends of Old Blaye) suggest that Blaye was named because it was on a military road: the *belli via*, or "war road," in Latin. But the *Dictionnaire étymologique des noms de lieux en France* instead suggests that, although it had been Latinized, the name had Gaulish origins. In this case, the Latin wouldn't have been *belli via* but *Blavius*, perhaps from a Gaulish personal name. There is also a suggestion that this name could have evolved from a Gaulish word, *blavos*, meaning "yellow."

PRIMITIVO • This Italian name for the Zinfandel grape (originating in Croatia as *Crljenak Kaštelanski*) is said to have been applied by Don Francesco Filippo Indellicati, a priest working in viticulture in the late 1700s. Comparing vines from mixed vineyards, he noted that this grape ripened first. The name *Primitivo* thus reflects the etymology of *prime*, meaning "first," as opposed to a "rough," "simple," or "rustic" sense that one might associate with the English word *primitive*.

PROHIBITION • The years 1920 to 1933 were the time of Prohibition in the United States. The root of *prohibition* is the word *prohibit*, which English got directly from Latin during the early part of the Renaissance, when classical knowledge was being rediscovered and Latin was seen as the language of scholarship. The Latin word in turn was built on two parts: *pro*, meaning "before" or "in front of," and *habere*, meaning "to have" or "to hold." Thus, to prohibit something is literally to block someone from having it.

PROLES • Grapevines are divided into species, such as the wild vines *Vitis riparia* and *Vitis rupestris* and the favored wine-producing *Vitis vinifera*. Within *Vitis vinifera*, there are thousands of varieties familiar to us as Pinot Noir, Chardonnay, and the rest. These thousands of varieties are further subdivided into three proles: *occidentalis*, *pontica*, and *orientalis*. The first one makes up the bulk of wine-producing grapes, but the division is actually driven by geography; the three home regions are progressively eastward, as implied by the third, *orientalis*. The term *proles* is singular, so one of them would not be a *prole*. It is a Latin word meaning "race" or "breed" and is the root of the Soviet-sounding *proletariat*.

PROPAGATION • *The Oxford Companion to Wine* defines the current meaning of *propagation* as "the reproduction of a plant, whether by sexual or asexual means." That doesn't reveal the fact that the word is actually rooted in wine history. The etymology of *propagate* points unerringly not only to the reproduction of vines but also to asexual reproduction. In Classical Latin, *propago* referred generally to grafting plant shoots for propagation, but most often and most strongly to this kind of botanical management for grapevines. *Propago* was formed on two parts; *pro*, meaning "forward" or "forth," and *pago*, meaning "to fasten," as one would do in grafting a shoot. Thus, *propagation* literally means "going forth by fastening" and, more figuratively, "continuing the plant by grafting." It is also the root for the word *propaganda*, which came to English in the late 1600s from Roman Catholic evangelists who had taken the botanical term as a metaphor

139

and called their group *Congregatio de propaganda fide* or "congregation for propagating the faith."

PROVENCE • The southeast corner of France is called *Provence* because the Romans called any territory outside their geographic Italian base *provincia*. In the case of Provence, the territory was the first area west of the Alps to come under Roman rule. Folk etymology assigns *pro*, meaning "before," and *vincere*, meaning "conquer," as the roots of *Provence* but etymologists have made no such link.

PUGLIA • Puglia is the portion of Italy that represents the heel of its "boot" and extends northwest up the Adriatic coast. This Italian name is recognized as *Apulia* in English and came from the Greek name for the area.

PULL • Although the etymology of *pull* is a little hazy, the most likely word history does make it appropriate for the pulling of corks. It is an Old English word and may have come from Frisian, the language of one of the Germanic tribes that took over Britain with the Angles and Saxons about 1500 years ago. The word's possible Frisian parent meant "to husk" or "to hull," as one would do to peas; thus, the word is etymologically applicable to the removal of the covering between you and the wine.

PUNT • The hollow in the bottom of a wine bottle is called the *punt*. This name appeared in English in 1862, only one year after the word *kick* was used to describe the same bottle feature. The best guess as to why this indentation might be called a *punt* is that an instrument used to make bottles was also called a *punt* or a *pontil*. It was an iron bar that in turn got its name from French, where its etymology means "little point." The tool was used to hold the molten glass blob as it was being formed into a bottle. As such, it left a scar on the finished bottle that was often ground off, leaving a slight indentation.

Q

QUALITY • This word is usually used to describe things, including wines, that are superior to others. The word entered English from French after the Norman Conquest and at first referred to the "nature" or "kind" of something; wine would thus have been of red or white quality. It was only later that *quality* implied a relative standard of excellence between things of the same kind. Before French, the Latin word *qualis* meant "of what sort?" and was built on *qui*, meaning "who."

QUEENSLAND • This Australian state was once administratively part of New South Wales and referred to as Moreton Bay District. When it was established as a state, the names Cooksland, Flinders, and Flindersland were considered before Queen Victoria put in her request that it be named in her honor. Flinders had been a popular name based on one Matthew Flinders, who had been an explorer in the early 1800s.

QUINCY • This French wine area in the Loire Valley south of Orleans likely takes its name from a Roman personal name, Quintius.

QUINTA • *Quinta* is a term used in Portuguese to refer to a farm and may be included in the names of wine producers. The word arose from the Latin word *quintus*, meaning "fifth," because these farms were rented out at a rate of one fifth of the revenue they generated.

R

RABOSO • According to *The Oxford Companion to Wine*, this Italian variety of red grape gets its name from the Italian word *rabbioso*, meaning "angry," a word closely related to the English word *rabies*. The assumption in *The Oxford Companion to Wine* is that the anger is on the part of wine drinkers reacting to high levels of tannins and acidity in the resulting wine. However, it may also be possible that the wine itself might be termed *angry*, due to these taste characteristics. *Angry* has certainly been used in this way in English; *The Oxford English Dictionary* notes that *angry* has meant "sharp, acrid in taste" from as early as the 14th century.

RAISIN • Just as the English word *grape* now means a single berry but used to mean an entire bunch of berries, the word *raisin* came to English via French from a Latin word, *racemus*, that meant an entire bunch of grapes. The English sense of *raisin* as a dried grape was already being adopted in French during the 1300s, although modern French recognizes the word as referring to both the fresh and dried fruits.

RED • This most basic designation of wine type is also one of the most basic of words. Solidly Old English as *read*, the word has relatives in Germanic languages as well as in a number of other languages that inherited it from its Indo-European base, *reudh*. (See **Paso Robles**, p. 132.)

REGURGITATE • The existence of a word like *regurgitate* implies the existence of another word, *gurgitate*. Sure enough, there it is in *The Oxford English Dictionary*, along with *ingurgitate*. Both at one time meant "to swallow" and, particularly, "to drink," sometimes excessively. Yet to the extent that this unusual word *gurgitate* is still used (there is one reference as recent as 1963), it is now supposed to mean "swallowed up as if dropped into a whirlpool." And it is from *whirlpool* that all these words come, because the Latin word for whirlpool was *gurges*. The first time the word *regurgitate* was used in English—as far as we can tell from the written record—was by Henry More in 1653. It was one of those instances where old Latin words were being drawn into use in English by great thinkers trying to express ideas that they found hard to articulate using only English words. More wasn't talking about human regurgitation but about fluid flow. It wasn't until 1753 that *regurgitate* was used to describe vomiting.

REHOBOAM • A bottle capable of containing 4.5 liters of wine or the equivalent of six standard bottles, a Rehoboam is named after a king of Judah who also happened to be the son of the wise Solomon. This designation appeared in 1895 in English.

REIMS • The epicenter of Champagne, the city of Reims takes its name from a Gaulish tribe who called themselves *Remi*, meaning "dominant ones."

RESERVE • A word supposedly used to designate better wines, as if they were being held back as something special. The fact that the term is used for marketing purposes more than as a true endorsement of quality is a double insult to the etymology of the word. *Reserve* was once in Latin *re-servare*, and since *servare* itself meant "to keep," the *re* prefix amplified this desirability.

RETSINA • The taste of retsina is a taste of antiquity. The name of this Greek white wine is taken from the word *resin*, because it is the resin of pine trees that gives retsina its particular taste. Thousands of years ago, when wine was fermented, stored, and shipped in pottery amphorae, pine resin was used to seal these porous vessels, reducing evaporation and prolonging the shelf life of the wine. Ancient drinkers grew accustomed to the taste of the resin in the wine

144

and even after amphorae fell out of use 2000 years ago, Greek drinkers in particular took to adding a little resin to the wine so they could enjoy the taste they'd grown accustomed to.

RHINE and RHÔNE • The names of these two rivers both ultimately mean "river." They may come from an Indo-European root, *rei*, meaning to "run" or "flow," that is thought to have also given English *runnel*, "a small stream," via Old English.

RIESLING • The word *Riesling* unequivocally appeared in print in 1552. It was originally a German word for a type of grape. Earlier appearances that might have represented different spellings of *Riesling* had occurred, but it is possible that these referred to a different grape type now known as *Räuschling*. There is no credible trail showing where the name *Riesling* came from, but the 1552 document where it first appeared is of some interest. Hieronymus Bock was the author of this book about the plants he found around him in Germany. Aside from being the first person to document the word *Riesling*, Bock is remembered as a father of botany. He had worked as a groundskeeper for some years, developing his love of growing things. When he decided to write a book detailing the various aspects of plants, he found himself unable to afford the cost of illustrations. So, instead, he turned to minute verbal description. Although academic texts were still commonly written in Latin, Bock wrote at first in the common German dialect that he used every day. That resulted in an excellent record of the language of his time and place. Things worked out well and the book went through several editions, many of them with illustrations. The book was also translated into Latin, and it is in a Latin edition that *Riesling* first appeared.

RIOJA • The major Spanish wine region takes its name from *Rio Oja*, meaning "Oja River." The origin of the name *Oja* is disputed, with some claiming it to be of Basque and others of

Latin origin. Within Rioja are the three wine regions of Alta, Alavesa, and Baja. *Alta* is Spanish for "high" from the Latin *altus*, the same root that gave English the word *altitude*. *Alavesa* denotes the province of Alava, a name that means "among the mountains," from the Basque word *araiiar*. *Baja* is Spanish for "low" and comes from the Latin *bassus*; this Latin word traces further back to the Greek word for "step."

RIPE • Wines are said to be best when the grapes that they were made from were given enough time to become fully ripe on the vine. That wasn't and isn't always the case, since growers face risks of adverse weather. Just as their crop grows toward its highest value, so too does its risk of destruction increase. The word *ripe* fits right in with this time of harvest; it's an Old English word that grew out of *reap*, meaning "harvest."

ROCKPILE • This American Viticultural Area is named because in 1867, Sheriff Tennessee Carter Bishop named his California ranch *Rockpile* and the location became the vineyard. Local legend has it that the reason for his choice of name was that he used prison labor to hack a road up to the ranch. When he was asked what work the prisoners were doing, his response was, "They're working on the rock pile."

ROMANIA • Wine has been produced in what is now Romania since the time of Classical Greece, and Romania is the largest wine producer in Eastern Europe. It may seem curious that Romania is named because the occupants felt it was the land of the Romans. The logic of this etymology is that a people known as the *Dacians* occupied Romania and were building their own empire in parallel with the Romans. That attracted the attention of the Romans during their drive toward world domination, so they brought out the big guns and took over the place. The Romans intensively integrated with the locals, so that eventually practically all the residents identified themselves as Roman.

146

ROOT • This physical connection of vines to soil has a name with surprisingly deep and branching origins. The Indo-European base word was *wrad*, which came to Old English as *wrot*. It was related to another English word, *wort*, that meant "plant" or "herb" and that still appears as part of the folk names of such plants as St. John's wort or bladderwort. The application of *wort* as a designator was particularly indicative of the plant's perceived usefulness in cooking or medicine. As such, the etymology of *root* has unexpectedly strong connections to another meaning of the word *wort*: wort is the unfermented precursor of beer, as must is to wine. This connection to plant derived aromatics and flavor also gives us the first element of the grape name *Gewürztraminer*, since *Gewürz* (meaning "spice") evolved from *wurz*, which also meant "plant" or "root" and derives from the same Indo-European origin as *root*. (See **Gewürztraminer**, p. 86.)

ROSÉ • *Pink wine* does not sound like a very good name for marketing purposes. Perhaps we should translate it into French? Of course, the French *rosé* came already named into English and no marketing manager had to invent it, but it does indeed mean "pink" in French. While the flower called a *rose* was named back in Old English with citations back to the year 888, *rosé* the wine designation didn't show up in English until more than a thousand years later, in 1897. The flower name runs back through Latin and Greek and may ultimately come from an Indo-European word meaning "thorn" or "bramble." The color *rosé* took its French name from the Latin *rosa*, which in turn came from the flower. That 1897 citation for *rosé* comes from an interesting source: a letter from Aubrey Beardsley to Leonard Smithers. Beardsley was an illustrator who gained fame when Oscar Wilde noticed his work. Smithers was a publisher. Both Beardsley and Smithers were accused at various times of being pornographers. The actual document that first mentions rosé wine is a cover letter under which Beardsley was shipping some artwork from Paris to Smithers in London. In a friendly closing note, Beardsley quipped that he had been unable to keep his meals down over the past several days, and so the rosé wine that Smithers had served him had been avenged.

ROUSSANNE • This grape name is closely connected to *rousse* and *rouge*, the French words for "red."

ROUSSILLON • Roussillon is a winegrowing region at the extreme southwestern end of the French Mediterranean coastline. It takes its name from Latin *Ruscino*, which was also the name of its former capital city. The source of this name is speculated to be the Semitic word *rosh*, meaning "head" or "cape." This root also appears in the name of the Jewish New Year, *Rosh Hashanah*, which translates as "head of the year."

RUSSIAN RIVER • This Sonoma County, California, wine area takes its name from the Russian settlement at Fort Ross. The Russians themselves called the river *Slavianka*, meaning "slave woman," and the Spanish had earlier dubbed it *San Ygnacio* after St. Ignatius of Loyola, founder of the Society of Jesus, otherwise known as the *Jesuits*. By 1843, however, the Spanish name had begun to turn to *Rio Ruso*, and in 1852 it was mapped as the *Russian River*. (See **Fort Ross**, p. 80.)

RUTHERFORD • This town in the Napa Valley was named after Thomas Rutherford, who acquired land as a wedding gift when he married Elizabeth Yount in 1864. The land was given by Elizabeth's grandfather, George Yount, who also gave nearby Yountville its name. By the 1880s, a railway station and post office had taken on the name *Rutherford*. Rutherford was himself a grape grower and wine producer. The name *Rutherford* may come from a place name formed from a Celtic word meaning "swift" plus *ford*, meaning a place where a river may be crossed.

S

SALMANAZAR • Shalmanazar was the name of a series of kings of Assyria approximately 3000 years ago. In 1935, this name became associated in English with a nine-liter wine bottle that can contain the equivalent of 12 standard bottles.

SAN JOAQUIN VALLEY • Gabriel Moraga, a Spanish army officer who explored the southern portion of California's central valley, gave it this name around 1805. *San Joaquin* refers to the sainted father of Mary, mother of Jesus. The name *Joaquin* comes from Hebrew and means "God prepares."

SAN LUIS OBISPO • This winegrowing county in California—whose name translates into English as "St. Louis, the Bishop," and which is known locally as "SLO"—was named for the mission founded there in 1772. The mission in turn was named in honor of St. Louis, bishop of Toulouse, France, in the late 1200s. Louis wasn't so much a great bishop as he was a reluctant king. He was the second son of Charles the Lame, king of Naples, who had bartered for his own freedom by ransoming his three sons. That wasn't as ghastly as it might seem, since the brothers were still treated like princes and raised by monks. At the age of 20, while still in captivity, the pope gave Louis administrative control over the archbishopric of Lyon. Both his father and older brother died, so the kingdom of Naples fell to him, but upon his release at age 21 he renounced his title and gave it to his younger brother, preferring instead to pursue a career in the church. He was made bishop of Toulouse at age 22 but died before reaching 23.

SANGIOVESE • This red wine grape is the most widely planted vine type in Italy. The name *Sangiovese* translates as "blood of Jove" and is thought to appear in Italian literature as early as 1590 as *Sangioghcto*. *Blood of Jove* is a particularly attractive name for a wine, encapsulating as it does the wine's color plus the spiritual elevation one might experience after a glass or two. *Jove* is a most ancient Latin name for the god Jupiter. *Jupiter* evolved out of *Jovis-pater*, meaning "Jove the father," since Jove was king of the gods. The potential antiquity of the grape name led many to think that the variety itself might date from classical winemaking times. The results of DNA testing and other evidence indicate a more recent appearance; likely sometime prior to 1700, making the 1590 date possible. However, it is also possible that the 1590 citation assigned this attractive name to some other grape variety.

SANGRIA • The name of this famous Spanish wine punch literally means "bleeding," which likely refers to the color imparted by red wine, one of its key ingredients. The word didn't appear in English with the Spanish spelling until 1961, but *sangaree* was first cited in 1736 as the name of a popular if lowbrow punch. At least two dictionaries of slang included *sangaree* before 1800 and defined it as "rack punch," *rack* being a shortening of *arrak* and referring to alcoholic drinks made from any number of foodstuffs, from rice to palm sap. Evidently then, as now, sangria recipes called for a very modest investment in ingredients.

SANTA BARBARA • This California winegrowing area takes its name from the city of Santa Barbara, which in turn takes its name from the Santa Barbara Channel running between the coast and the Channel Islands. This channel was named by Sebastián Vizcaíno, a Spanish explorer who stopped here on December 4, 1602. December 4th happened to be the feast day of St. Barbara, which is why he chose the name. St. Barbara had a hard time of it historically and isn't faring much better today. During her lifetime, thought to possibly have been around the year 300, Christianity was only just beginning to become popular. It wasn't popular with her father,

150

however. When she converted to Christianity, he contacted the authorities, who gave him permission to behead her. Although she herself had become popular by Sebastián Vizcaíno's time, her popularity then faded within the Catholic Church for the simple reason that there is little documentary evidence to prove she actually existed. She is thus no longer officially recognized as a saint. There is one bright spot, however: on his way home from the execution, Barbara's father is said to have been hit by lightning.

SANTA CLARA VALLEY • Santa Clara doesn't mean what it used to. Once a storied winegrowing valley, it is now more commonly known as *Silicon Valley*. The valley was named *Santa Clara* after St. Clare of Assisi, one of Francis of Assisi's early disciples. The riches of the computer industry represent quite a change from the sense of poverty that Santa Clara once conveyed. The Order of Poor Ladies that St. Clare founded was like the Franciscan order and pledged to poverty; it was later known as the Poor Clares. The valley was named by Juan Crespí, a Spanish missionary and explorer who visited it in 1769. He is an important source of information on early California history because he wrote the first accounts of interaction between Franciscans and the native indigenous population already living in the area.

SANTA CRUZ • This California wine region takes its name from the city of Santa Cruz. In 1769, an expedition by Gaspar de Portolà i Rovira encountered what is now known as Majors Mill Creek and named it *Santa Cruz*, and it is from this stream that the city takes its name. The Spanish explorers named many places *Santa Cruz*–literally, "holy cross." The fact that *santa* in this case translates to "holy" instead of "saint" points out the different heritages of these two English words. *Holy* was an Old English word that was retained in English even after *saint* arrived, likely because the word *holy* itself was held in such high esteem. Yet *saint* was originally synonymous with *holy*; it didn't mean "a holy person." The Latin root of

151

saint was *sacer*, meaning "holy," and that is where we also get the word *sacred*. The Spanish word *cruz* also shines light on an aspect of English etymology. The vast majority of Modern English words with Latin roots came into English after 1066, either with the French of the Norman Conquest or, later, directly from scholarly Latin. A very small number of Latin words found their way into Old English, and *cross* is one of these. It was the spread of Christianity and the English adoption of church Latin that planted these early Latin words. *Cross* is a particularly churchy word and it displaced the Old English word *rood*.

SANTA MARIA VALLEY • You'd think the name of this California valley in Santa Barbara County would be an easy one to trace, since Mary was the mother of Jesus. That is very likely why there are so many places called Santa Maria: people thought it referred to that particular Mary. However, the Spanish usually called her *Nuestra Senora*, meaning "Our Lady," rather than *Santa Maria*. For this reason, some suspect that the Mary named in *Santa Maria* must have been some other St. Mary. There are quite a few candidates for this other Mary, including Mary Magdalene, Mary Salome, Mary of Egypt, Mary of Alexandria, Mary of Cerevellon, and Mary Frances.

SANTA RITA HILLS • There are a number of places in California with the *Santa Rita* moniker but only the one appended to hills in Santa Barbara County is a winegrowing region. The saint being remembered is St. Rita of Cascia, *Rita* being a shortening of *Margherita*, a popular medieval name going back through the Greek *margaron,* meaning "pearl," and thought to have originated in Hebrew before that. St. Rita has a biography that makes you wonder about the criteria for sainthood. Forced to marry at 12, she endured a violent, abusive husband who eventually died after a knife fight. Rita had been working him around to religious conversion, however, and so when the end was nigh, he repented and Rita forgave him. Rita had two sons and they vowed to get revenge for their father's death. Rita tried to talk them out of it, but when they insisted on carrying it out, she prayed to God to prevent their impending sin—by killing them. What's a mother to do? Evidently, the church debated how exactly she fit the criteria for sainthood, since it took 170 years to beatify her and then another 270 years before she was canonized.

SANTA YNEZ VALLEY • This California wine area was first dubbed with the names of two other saints by explorers before it finally got its current name with the establishment of the Santa Ynez mission in 1804. *Santa Ynez* is "St. Agnes" to English speakers, a saint from roughly the year 300 who was extremely popular in the Middle Ages. Her sainthood is due to her martyrdom as a virgin; that and the fact that she was only 12 or 13 are about the only things that the ancient accounts agree on. Some say she was forced into a brothel, where her hair grew to hide her nakedness; others say that visitors to the brothel were struck blind when they looked at her. Her name *Agnes* comes from the Greek name *Hagne* and means "pure" or "holy." Christianity has long analogized the guiding shepherd and his flock and the chance similarity of *agnus*, the Latin word for "lamb," is thought to have contributed to the transformation from *Hagne* to *Agnes*.

SAUTERNES • The dictionaries note that the name of this sweet Bordeaux white was documented a century earlier in English than in French; *The Oxford English Dictionary* reports a first citation in 1711 and the *Petit Robert* in 1814. The wine is certainly named after the place name of a village that is far older. Several theories are offered for its etymology. In Latin, *saltu terra* is thought to have meant "wooded terrain"; *salva terra*, meaning "land of refuge," has also been suggested as the source of *Sauternes*. Finally, a Celtic origin has been theorized, from *sau* (meaning "mound") and *ternevan* (meaning "embankment").

SAUVIGNON • *Sauvignon* appears in several grape names, most famously as *Cabernet Sauvignon* but also alone as *Sauvignon*, also known as *Sauvignon Blanc*; as *Sauvignon Gris* and *Sauvignon Rose*, which are the same grape variety; within *Sauvignonasse*, also known as *Sauvignon Vert*; and even as *Sauvignon Rouge*. Pierre Rézeau's *Dictionnaire des noms de cépages de France* indicates that the word *Sauvignon* appeared in French documents as early as 1690, applied first to a black grape type. The word didn't turn up in English before the 19th century and left little trace of where it came from in either French or English. Claims have been made that *Sauvignon* is related to the French word *sauvage*, meaning "wild." Rézeau does find corroborative evidence for this theory in an alternative name, *Fié gris*, that may have evolved from the Latin *férus*, also meaning "wild." However, Rézeau concurs with other French and English etymology sources in concluding that the evidence for a link between *Sauvignon* and *sauvage* is inconclusive.

SAVOIE • This mountainous eastern French wine region is known in English as Savoy but was known in Latin as *Sapaudia*. Some theorize that the Latin name may have once meant "covered in fir trees," based on the Latin word *sapinus*, meaning "fir tree."

SCUPPERNONG • This native North American grape appears to have a native North American name. The grapes were brought to public attention in 1810 by one James Blount and given the name *Scuppernong* by one Calvin Jones, who shared credit for the naming with a Mr. Henderson. The name was awarded based on the fact that James Blount was a resident of the North Carolina town of Scuppernong, plus the belief that these grapes grew especially well along the small Scuppernong River. The etymology of the river's name is uncertain but it is assumed to be a native North American Indian name.

SÉMILLON • The name *Sémillon* had appeared by 1736 in French and by 1875 in English. Etymological sources agree that the name of this grape type comes from planting. Strictly speaking, the Latin word *semen* meant "seed," but its meaning extended also to shoots and cuttings. From this Latin root sprang, in the dialect of what is now southern France, the word *semilhar*, meaning "to sow." A second, less highly regarded theory on the etymology claims that the name is a contraction of St-Émilion, the name of the city in Bordeaux. This origin is suggested in the first French citation for *Sémillon* in 1736.

SHENANDOAH VALLEY • A little confusingly, there are two Shenandoah valleys and both have American Viticultural Area designations. The one in California is said to have been named by John Jameson for his birthplace, which was the other Shenandoah Valley in Virginia. The one in Virginia is named from an Algonquin word meaning "spruce stream."

SHERRY • This fortified white wine takes its name in English from the Spanish city where it originated. Now known as *Jerez*, the city was previously called *Xeres*. The word *Sherries*, meaning the "wine of Xeres" appears first in English around 1540 in a will that leaves—among other things—"twenty buttes of sakes of Sherries." English speakers, having made the error of thinking *Sherries* meant the wine itself instead of *Xeres* (the place it came from), compounded their error by assuming *Sherries* (*Xeres*) was the plural of *sherry*. The city of Jerez has a particularly ancient wine tradition, possibly over 3000 years old. One claim that seems unsubstantiated is that this viticultural success led to the city's name *Jerez* being applied after Ceres, another wine-producing city in what is now Italy. The "sakes" mentioned in "buttes of sakes of Sherries" in 1540 refers to *sack*, an obsolete wine word. *Sack* was a name for white wines coming from Spain and the Canary Islands as early as the 1530s and is believed to be a derivation from the French *vin sec*, meaning "dry wine."

However, a mystery surrounds this etymology in that these wines are thought to have been sweet not dry.

SHIRAZ • The Shiraz grape takes its name from a confused tumble of history. The earliest modern use of the name was in relation to a shipment of vines brought from France to Australia by James Busby in the early 1800s. Absolute identification of grape types and connections to unique names are not universal even today. In Busby's time, things were even less precise, and his Shiraz cuttings arrived under several different names. In France, the very same vine type also went by different names, or at least spellings: *Syrah, Scyras* and *Sirrah* were known. Although some might think that the word *Shiraz* is a kind of corruption of one of these French names, in fact, around 100 years ago, people were instead contending that the name *Syrah* and its variants were corruptions of *Shiraz.* This topsy-turvy logic arose because there had been a fabled wine called *Shiraz* in medieval times, named after the city of Shiraz in modern-day Iran. This ancient wine does seem to have existed and inspired a myth in the Rhône that vines brought back during the time of the Crusades were now growing as *Syrah.* Besides the fact that the ancient wine of Shiraz was white and modern Shiraz is red, DNA testing has crushed the Iranian theory and instead supports Syrah as a native of France. The same testing confirms that Syrah is indeed identical to the Shiraz grown in Australia and elsewhere. Although the city of Shiraz is unlikely to be responsible for this collection of grape names, it does indeed have a strong wine-related history. The city of Shiraz is thought to be named for two Elamite words: *sher,* meaning "good," and *raz,* meaning "grape." (See **Syrah,** p. 163.)

SIERRA FOOTHILLS • The Sierra Foothills, a California wine region, are named for the obvious reason of their proximity to the Sierra Nevada mountain range. The word *sierra* is Spanish for "saw," and the jagged peaks of the ranges reminded people of the teeth of a saw and lent the name to the mountain range. The Latin *serra* also meant "saw," and we see this root in our English word *serrated*. *Nevada* is also a Spanish word and means "snow"; it came from the Latin *nix* or *niv*, also meaning "snow." The "n" in *nix* and in *snow* likely points to an ancient etymological relationship.

SILVANER or **SYLVANER** • All etymological sources invoke *Silvanus* the Roman god of woods and trees as the root of the German grape name *Silvaner*. Some sources consider this as indicative that this variety had originally been growing wild. Based on the *Silvanus* etymology, plus a purported long history for Silvaner in Eastern Europe, others suggest that the grape may have originated in Transylvania. Although Transylvania may be famous in the West as a semi-mythical place that Count Dracula called home, it is in fact a historical location covering roughly half of present-day Romania. The name *Transylvania* is from Medieval Latin and means "beyond the forest."

SIRAH • Appearing predominantly in *Petite Sirah*, the name is first documented in French as *Petite Scyras* in 1827 or earlier, but found greater fame in California after the 1880s. Although Petite Sirah may inherit its name from Syrah, it isn't the same grape…usually. DNA testing in 1997 showed that vines called *Petite Sirah* actually comprised four different varieties, including Syrah. (See **Shiraz**, p. 156, and **Syrah**, p. 163.)

SKIN • The skins of grapes are important in winemaking for the color and flavor they impart to the wine. The word *skin* came to us from our carnivorous diet and the days of the Vikings. The Indo-European root was *sek* and meant "cut." It arrived via Germanic roots in Old Norse as *skinn* and the "cutting" meaning was relevant because the skin of an animal was cut away from the carcass. *Skin* didn't appear in writing in English until around the year 1200, because it was a word used in the north by the descendants of the Vikings who established the area known as the Danelaw. It took time both for literacy to be established there and for their northern dialects to integrate into what was becoming "standard English."

SLOPE • Sloping land in vineyards is important in terms of both its orientation to sunshine and of the way night air moves over the vines forming warmer or cooler pockets, depending on the site. The word *slope* appeared less than 400 years ago in English and the evidence as to how it got there is somewhat speculative. It is supposed that it was a shortening of an earlier word, *aslope*, describing something that was sloping and dating from 1400. This in turn is thought to relate to the word *slip*, but if the two are indeed related, the evidence linking the two—a theoretical word, *aslupcan*—either was never written down or has been lost over the centuries.

SOAVE • Soave is a wine region in northeastern Italy. Although the Italian word *soave* holds a meaning of "smooth," "sweet," or "delightful" and evolved from the Latin *suavis*, the use of the term to apply to wine from the Soave region is coincidental. The wine term comes instead from the historic name of the region, which was named for the Suevian Germanic tribes who troubled the Roman Empire from the north.

SOIL • An important component of many wines is *terroir*, which in turn is heavily influenced by the soil of a vineyard. The word *soil* came to English with a meaning of "earth" or "ground" but with an etymology verging on "estate" or "property." The French word, adopted into English in the 14th century, came from the Latin word *solium*, but *solium* had meant "seat" and sometimes "throne." Thus, *soil* sometimes even took on a meaning of "homeland." However, there was another Latin word, *solum*, that meant "floor" and "ground." People applied the meaning of the latter to the former, so we came to view *soil* as referring to the material into which plants send their roots.

SOMMELIER • The word used to describe a waiter with specialized knowledge of wine arrived in English in *Harper's Magazine* in 1889. French had been using the term in this way since 1812. Yet the professional title is cited in *The Oxford English Dictionary* as meaning a "butler" as early as 1543. Back in ancient Greek, "to pack" was *sattien.* Latin is thought to have picked this word up and integrated it into *sagma,* a word meaning "packsaddle," and *sagmarius,* "having to do with beasts of burden." When Latin became French, a *sommier* became a "pack animal" and a *sommerier* was their handler. Although the connection between *butler* and wine is clear, the reason that a manager of pack animals should evolve into a wine specialist is less obvious. One hint may lie in that first 1543 citation for the Anglicized *somler.* Therein, the sommelier is clearly identified as the person responsible for overseeing and accompanying a wine shipment. (See **butler,** p. 31.)

SONOMA • In 1849, the California senate established Sonoma as a county along with numerous others. In 1850, a report was published explaining the origins of the names of these new counties. In this report, *Sonoma* was said to have originated as an Indian word meaning "valley of the moon." But subsequent researchers have argued that if the name signified "valley of the moon," it would have been rendered *Sanoma.* The evidence appears to lean in a less romantic but perhaps more charming etymological direction. The earliest evidence comes from baptismal records of 1814, where the word is rendered as the name of a tribe as *Sonomas* and subsequently as *Sonomi.* Instead of meaning "moon," *sono* likely means "nose" in the native Patwin language. It's speculated that the name "nose valley" got attached to the place because a local native chief possessed a proboscis of notable proportions. According to one anecdote, such a chief was named "nose" at birth, according to a native custom whereby names were given according to notable features.

SOVEREIGN • A sovereign wine bottle is sized to hold the equivalent of 34 standard bottles. The word *sovereign*, meaning "king," came to English from French and Latin, where it is thought to have been *superanus*, from *superans* meaning "dominant," from *super*, meaning "above."

SPAIN • The Spanish call Spain *Espana*, and there are three competing theories as to the origin of the name. *Hesperus*, a Greek word, means "of the evening" and refers to the westerly direction of the setting sun; Spain is one of the westernmost points in Europe, save Portugal. In a similar sense with a more indigenous language root, the Basque word *ezpain* or *ezpan* means "edge." Finally, the North African Punic word *span* meant "rabbit" and is claimed by some to have been applied because there was once an abundance of rabbits in Spain. (Don't laugh; that's how Coney Island got its name.)

SPARKLING • A *spark* is identified as a small particle of fire in glosses as far back as the year 725, and *sparkle* was attributed to wine as early as 1422, long before wines were designed to effervesce. Wine is called sparkling based on its light-reflecting qualities. Some sources link the Old English *spearca* to the Latin *spargere*, meaning "to scatter," as sparks from a fire might do. That word in turn is linked to the Greek *spargan*, meaning "to swell," which also appears unexpectedly in English in the word *asparagus*.

SPRITZER • This name for a mixture of wine and soda water appeared for the first time in English in *Vogue Magazine* in 1961. In German, *spritzer* means "splash."

SPUMANTE • In Italian, *spumante* means "sparkling" and comes from the Latin *spuma*, meaning "foam." From the same root, sailors may get sprayed with foam from the sea called *spume* or diners at an Italian restaurant may enjoy a kind of ice cream called *spumoni*.

ST-ÉMILION • The Bordeaux area of St-Émilion takes its name from the city of St-Émilion, which in turn takes its name from an 8ᵗʰ century religious hermit who inhabited a cave there. Upon the site, a cathedral has grown and the cave has been expanded upon enormously.

STAGS LEAP • Grapes have been grown in the California wine area that has become the Stags Leap District since before the first winery was established in 1878. The man credited with the *Stags Leap* name was Horace Chase, who began operations in 1888 and in 1893 produced wine labeled as being from the Stags Leap Winery. He is said to have chosen the name based on a legend of deer escaping hunters by bounding between rocky ledges nearby. The Stags Leap name and region came to prominence in 1976 when one of the region's wines—a 1973 Cabernet Sauvignon, made by Stags Leap Wine Cellars—won a blind taste tasting by French judges in Paris, in competition with French wines of the first rank. In 1986, in a repeat of the famed "Judgment of Paris" tasting, another wine from the Stags Leap District took top honors: the 1973 Clos Du Val Cabernet Sauvignon.

STANDARD • Bottles of various sizes are given names such as *Magnum*, *Methuselah*, and *Jeroboam* and are compared with the capacity of a "standard" 750-milliliter bottle. Yet the workhorse "standard" bottle has no name. The word *standard* came into English in 1154 from French, where it had been *estandard*. The first meaning was "royal flag," such as might be unfurled during a battle, and the Latin etymology of *estandard* actually meant "extend" as is done with a flag in unfurling it. By the early 1400s, the royal authority associated with such a flag gave the word *standard* its own authority so that it signified "regulation size" as would be decreed by a sovereign.

STEM • The word *stem* is applicable to wine in at least four ways. Each grape is attached to a woody stock that might be called a *stem* but whose technical name is *pedicel,* meaning "little foot"; each bunch of grapes hangs on a stem also called a *bunchstem* and technically known as a *peduncle,* also meaning "little foot" (though perhaps not quite so little); new shoots on a vine are made up of a stem and leaves; and, finally, wine glasses are sometimes called *stemware* because they stand on stems. Of these meanings, it is the glass (and perhaps the shoot) that most closely relate to the etymology of *stem.* The Indo-European ancestor was *sta* and meant "stand," appearing in Old English as *stemn* or *stefn* as early as the year 888. *Stemware* is cited first in a Sears catalogue in the fall of 1929.

SUGAR • The sugars that feed the yeasts that produce alcohol in wine and the sugars that remain for us to taste are in liquid form, but the word *sugar* came about from the substance's appearance as a solid. In Sanskrit, *sharkara* meant "grit" or "gravel" and referred to the graininess of sugar in crystal form. This word made it into Arabic as *sukkar* and into Latin as *succarum.* The French of the Norman Conquest brought *sukere* to England.

SULFITES • Laws in some countries require labels on applicable wines to include the warning "contains sulfites." That is because sulfur dioxide is a long-established and widely used preservative in wine. The word *sulfur* came to English through French from Latin, but the English already had a name for the stuff. Sulfur dioxide is formed when sulfur is burned, and in ancient times sulfur was named for this ability to burn; *brimstone* literally means "burning stone."

SWEET • Wines are often described as sweet or dry. We usually associate more sweetness with an increasing quantity of sugar, but the complex combination of elements in wine and their interaction with our taste buds mean that, in fact, wines with higher sugar levels can sometimes taste dry, and wines with low levels of sugar can taste sweet. Appropriately, *swad*–the Indo-European root of the word *sweet*–didn't exclusively relate to sugary sweetness but also included a meaning of "pleasant." The word reached Old English as *swete* from a Germanic root, but the "pleasant" meaning also branched off and through Greek came into English in the word *hedonism*.

SWITZERLAND • Wine has certainly been produced in Switzerland for more than 2000 years. The name we use for the country is from the canton Schwyz, which formed the nucleus of a Swiss confederation beginning in 1291. The canton is named for the town of the same name within it. The town is thought to have been named *Suittes* originally, with a possible meaning related to the Old High German word *suedan*, meaning "to burn." If this etymology is accurate, the thinking is that the name arose from the use of fire in clearing the forests. Yet Switzerland does not call itself *Switzerland*. Because the country contains four different language groups and each of these renders the name of the nation a little differently, the official government name used is *Helvetia*, the name the Romans used for the area.

SYMPOSIUM • The modern meaning of *symposium* is slightly at variance with the ancient meaning. Today, a symposium is a kind of conference where the audience is largely made up of the same people who are speaking in one or another of the sessions. The objective is usually to exchange ideas among peers. In ancient Greece, a symposium did indeed involve the exchange of ideas among peers, but the very name of the event reveals that the objective was more the pursuit of pleasure than knowledge. Symposium breaks down into the Greek roots *sun* and *posis*, literally "together, to drink."

SYRAH • The first French citation for this grape name dates from 1781 as *sira*. There was a tradition that the name *Syrah* was applied because the grape had been brought to France from the city of Shiraz, capital of ancient Persia. An alternative tradition was that the vines originated in or were shipped from Syracuse on the island of Sicily. These two explanations are now seen to be folk etymologies, which is to say they sound attractive but have no supporting evidence. One alternative with less tradition but perhaps more merit is that the name comes ultimately from an Indo-European root *ser*, meaning "lengthy," which evolved into the Latin word *serus*, meaning "slow," which would have been applied to Syrah because the grape tends to ripen later than many other varieties. (See **Shiraz**, p. 156.)

T

TANNINS • Tannins have a complex relationship with wine. Grapes themselves have tannins, and winemakers may add other tannins by storing wine in wooden barrels or by using any number of other methods. Tannins can add bitterness or improve the taste and longevity of wine. Suffice it to say that tannins are important to winemaking, even though wine scientists haven't fully figured them out. The word *tannin* appeared in English in 1802, but the idea of tannins and the source of their name are much older. Leather has been tanned for thousands of years, and in being tanned it takes on a brownish color. This is why lying on the beach and turning your skin brown is called *tanning*. Ancient craftsmen crushed the bark of oak trees and extracted an infusion used to tan leather. The Latin word for tanning leather in this way was *tannare* but the root of the word may be a Celtic or Gaulish word, *tanno*, meaning "oak."

TASTE • The reason that wine has held a special place in human priorities for so many millennia is undoubtedly the fact that it mysteriously gave its drinkers those good feelings that alcohol can impart. But the care those ancient vignerons took in selecting the grape varieties that ultimately gave us *vinifera* was based primarily on the evidence of their tongues. Taste is what it's all about; taste is what it's always been about. But the word *taste* is a little bit mysterious in its etymology. Like so many other English words, *taste* came from French and from Latin before that, but in those languages and when it first arrived in English, it did not refer to the senses of the tongue; instead, *to taste* in 1292 meant "to touch." Just how a word describing the sensation of the fingertips might be reassigned to describe that of the mouth is unknown. But the precursor words to *taste* not only meant "touch" as in "make contact'" they also meant "touch" as in "explore" and "evaluate." This more highly qualitative "touch" may relate better to the complex sensations of our mouths.

TEETOTALER • A teetotaler is someone who does not drink any sort of alcoholic beverage. The term could not have appeared before the development of the temperance movement that arose in the early 1800s, since before that time there was little public mood for abstinence from beer, wine, or other alcoholic drinks. Accordingly, in 1834, we see the first appearance of "Tee-Total Abstainer." It's thought that the *tee* was there to give extra emphasis and highlight the depth of feeling of these non-drinking campaigners.

TEMECULA • This high desert California wine region's name is first cited as *Temeca* in 1785, then as *Temeco* in 1802 and finally as *Temecula* in 1820. There are arguments that *Temeco* was the original form, being the previous name of the Luiseño Indians. The meaning is unknown, but a root Luiseño Indian word—*temet*, meaning "sun"—has been suggested.

TEMPERANCE • The temperance movement emerged in the first half of the 1800s and has left us with the impression that *temperance* means "abstinence" from the consumption of alcohol. In fact, the temperance movement appropriated language in the same way pro-life and pro-choice advocates have carefully selected their labels. The word *temperance* was in use long before the 1800s. First appearing before 1340, the word was built on a French word that came ultimately from Latin. When translating Plato's four important virtues from Greek into Latin, the Roman Cicero included the Latin word for temperance as one of them; the others were prudence, fortitude, and justice. But what Cicero had in mind was moderation and self-control, not necessarily complete self-denial. The word *temperance* is related to the word *temper*, which in turn had a meaning of "balance" to it, as we still hear when we talk of people "losing their temper." Who could object to a social movement that advocated that people keep their emotions in balance?

TEMPRANILLO • The name of this highly thought-of Spanish grape variety comes from the Spanish word *temprano*, which means "early," so *Tempranillo* might be thought to mean "little early one." These grapes ripen ahead of many other types, thus earning their name. Like French, Spanish evolved when local languages mixed with Latin after the fall of the Roman Empire. As such, *temprano* has the same Latin roots as our word *temporary* and carries some of the same sense of "a short time." Some sources speculate that the deeper root of the Latin word for "time," *tempus*, could possibly be a prehistoric word, *ten*, meaning "stretch."

TENDRIL • The coiling shoots that vines extend to grasp and climb take their name from a Latin word, *tendere*, meaning "to stretch."

TERRACES • In some places, hillside vineyards are terraced. The technique breaks the slope into a series of flat shelves of land that can reduce erosion and make working the land more feasible. It is an expensive technique, so it's ironic that the word root denotes "a pile of rubble" and even "bad earth," "filthy earth," and "useless earth," according to *The Oxford English Dictionary*. The *ter* in *terrace* comes via the Latin *terra*, meaning "earth." It in turn came from an ancient Indo-European root, *ters*, meaning "dry" and denoting "dry land," presumably as opposed to the sea.

TERROIR • Although the now-popular French word *terroir* didn't appear as an English term describing the growing conditions of wine until 1968, the term *goût de terroir*, translating as "taste of the land," was used in English wine writing as early as 1893. *Terroir* comes from the Latin *territorium* and referred to the land around a town. The word root also lives on in the English word *territory*. These words also trace back to the Indo-European *ters*, meaning "dry" and by extension "dry land."

TOAST • People have been hoisting their glasses and drinking in honor of other people for many centuries. It is a tradition that goes back probably 1000 years in England and has deeper roots in Roman and Greek customs. For most of its history in English, this action was called "drinking a health." It was only about 200 years ago that people began referring to this little ceremony as "drinking a toast." There is little debate among the etymological sources as to the story behind this newer phrase; little debate, but no proof of accuracy. What is known for sure is that the word *toast* was in use in English for quite a while before it was applied to the drinking custom. Today, we think of toast as something made out of a slice of bread to be eaten in the morning. But for many centuries, *toast* instead meant smaller dried pieces of bread. For the longest time, it was customary to add spices to wine, and one of the ways of doing this was to spice pieces of toast and float them in the wine. The story goes that several people were enjoying the health-giving properties of the waters in the English city of Bath. As one of the ladies was bathing, an admirer dipped his glass into the water to drink her health. Another admirer expressed scorn for such a drink but said that he wouldn't mind at all the toast that was floating in it—that is, the girl.

TOKAY • This name has been attached to a number of wines and several different grape types in different places. For example, *Tokay d'Alsace* referred to *Pinot Gris* in Alsace, yet in Australia *Tokay* means *Muscadelle*, and in Friuli, Italy, *Sauvignonasse* is called *Tocai Friulano*. The relationship originates in *Tokaj*, the name of a town in northern Hungary and of the highly respected wines from that region dating back 400 years or more. That wine, called *Tokaji*, is made mainly from Furmint grapes. According to Adrian Room's *Placenames of the World*, two possibilities have been suggested for the origin of town's name. The Slavic word *tok* meant "current" and may have been applied based on the location of Tokaj at the confluence of the Bodrog and Tisza rivers. This etymology would depend on the name having been retained from sometime before the 9th century, when Slavs inhabited the area before being replaced by the Magyar, the people to whom modern Hungarians trace their roots. The second suggestion is that *Tokaj* evolved from a Turkic personal name.

TOURAINE • This important wine region in the Loire Valley is named for the *Turoni*, a Gaulish people whose name may come from a Celtic word meaning "powerful."

TRADITIONAL • Because makers of sparkling wines cannot call their wines *Champagne* unless it is made in a certain part of France, if they go to the trouble of making their bubbly by the most painstaking technique, they are allowed instead to say that it is made according to the *traditional method*. The word *tradition* is made up of two Latin components, *trans* and *dare,* with respective literal meanings of "across" and "hand," so that the figurative meaning is "to hand down," as this traditional technique is handed down from generation to generation.

TREBBIANO • A widely planted grape variety in Italy, it is named for the Trebbia River. This is the same grape type as Ugni Blanc.

TRELLIS • The trellis is the structure upon which vines are supported. From its Latin source, the word literally means "woven with three threads," but it was later applied to things made of woven metal or basketwork, which gave it a meaning of "lattice."

TRENTINO • The Italian region of Trentino takes its name from the city of Trento. The city name came from the Latin

Tridentum, meaning "three teeth," which was based on a mountain nearby with triple peaks.

TUSCANY • Tuscany in Italy is named for the ancient powerhouse people, the Etruscans. The Etruscans in turn took their name from the ancient name of their region, *Etruria,* which is thought to mean "water" and likely refers to the Arno and Tiber rivers.

U

UGNI • Ugni Blanc—a synonym for Trebbiano—is a very widely planted grape in France. The name *Ugni* is a contraction of the Latin *eugenia*, meaning "well born" or "noble." Originally a Greek name, it also gave us the personal name *Eugene*. The *gen* in the word is related to *gene* and *generation*.

ULLAGE • The word *ullage* can mean a number of things, but the one that's most visible to most wine drinkers is the space between the bottom of a cork and the top of the wine in an unopened wine bottle. That little air space is called the *ullage*. Old wines are likely to have a larger space, and sometimes old and valuable wines are topped up to reduce this exposure to air. It's the topping up that points to the etymology. *Ouillage* was an Old French word meaning "to fill up" and was usually applied to filling a barrel. Topping up a barrel was a more regular occurrence before the days of bottles and was done for the same reasons: wine would slowly evaporate through the pores of the wood, leaving an air space that could spoil the wine. It's the way the barrels were topped up that gave us the word: they were filled through the bunghole. The hole was likened to an eye, and the Old French word *ouil* meant "eye," from its Latin root, *oculus*.

UMBRIA • The Umbria region of Italy takes its name from the ancient Umbri people who lived there, who in turn took their name from the Umbro River. The name of the river may come from Greek and mean "rain" or "water."

UVA • The Latin and still Italian word for "grape" is closer than you think. At the back of your mouth, hanging down over your throat, is your uvula, which is Latin for "little grape."

V

VALENCIA • The Spanish wine region takes its name from the city of Valencia, which was known to the Romans as *Valentia Edetanorum*. The Edetani were the people who lived there and *valentia* was their "fort," from the Latin *valere*, meaning "strong."

VALLE D'AOSTA • This northwestern Italian wine region is named "valley of Aosta" after the city of Aosta. The city's name is a contraction of *Augusta Praetoria Salassorum*, the original name given by the Romans when they took over the local Salassi tribe during the rule of Emperor Augustus.

VALPOLICELLA • Most sources that offer an etymology for *Valpolicella* suggest that the word may be broken in three to form *vallis*, *poly*, and *cella*, to be translated as "valley of many cellars." This etymology may be true but is speculative. The region's name appears in the historical record in the 12th century, about the time when it fell under the influence of the then-independent city-state of Verona. Certainly, wine has been an important part of the economy of the area for thousands of years, but it isn't clear that it was so important that its cellars would have stood out among those of many other wine-producing areas to give the area its name. Several alternate etymologies have been suggested. One is that a port named *Pol*, now known as Santa Lucia di Pescantina, on the Adige River, gave the area its name translating as "valley downstream of Pol." Another possibility stems from the Latin word *sinus* which meant "curve," "bay," or "cavity." This etymology derives from the wanderings of the Adige River. The river's name comes from Indo-European roots meaning "fast river," and it pours out of the Val di Adige immediately to the west of Valpolicella before relaxing into the sinuous curves that meander just to the south of Valpolicella into Verona and beyond. *Sinus* in its form *sinuous*, renders

Valpolicella as "the valley of many curves (in the river)." Yet another etymology related to the river is suggested in the Latin word *pullus* meaning "dark colored" and offered as applying to the alluvial soils deposited by the slowing river flow. *Valpolicella* first appeared in English in 1903 in a book called *The Gourmet's Guide to Europe*, where it referred to the wine.

VARIETAL • It was Charles Darwin who introduced the word *varietal* to the world in 1866, in his *Origin of Species*. Darwin was using it in the most general of terms, applicable to any number of plants or animals. It was 1955 when the word was first specifically cited as applicable to wines made from a single type of grape. In both cases, however, the word is intended to distinguish a unique group from a broad variety of similar types of organisms. The parent word comes from the Latin *varietas*, meaning "difference" and "diversity."

VAT • Wines are fermented or stored in vessels sometimes called *vats*. Like the male and female words *fox* and *vixen*, the word *vat* is actually a southern variant of a word that in the north of England of 1000 years ago was *fat*. Old English speakers had their dialects, and what was an "f" in the north was often a "v" in the south. The Germanic root of both *vat* and this sense of *fat* meant "to hold." *Fat* shows up in *Beowulf*, but it took until 1225 before the southern *vat* was set to paper.

VEEDER • The California wine area known as Mount Veeder is named after Peter V. Veeder, a Presbyterian minister around 1860.

VENETO • The Italian region takes its name from the city of Venice, its capital. Venice itself is named for the original inhabitants, the Veniti.

174

VERAISON • The phase in the growing of grapes when the berries turn from a hard green and begin to gain their final color is called *veraison*. The word first appeared in French in 1826 and in English in 1889, and derives from the Latin *variare*. The same Latin word gave English *variegate*, which the *American Heritage Dictionary* defines as "to change the appearance of, especially by marking with different colors." That seems a remarkably applicable definition for *veraison* as well, due to the fact that some berries change color before others. Though *veraison* has been documented for less than 200 years, the *Robert* dictionary acknowledges it to be particularly old.

VERDOT • Although Petit Verdot grapes are a very dark color, the name *Verdot* actually comes from the French word *vert*, meaning "green." The reason for this is that they ripen late and the "green" doesn't so much refer to their color as to their unripened hardness and acidity late in the season, while other varieties are becoming sweet and juicy.

VERMENTINO • This grape name is mentioned in literature as early as 1825 but has no known etymology. That first mention was in Italian, and a Corsican citation appeared in 1837. Since the grape now referred to by this name turns from green to yellow as it ripens, one might speculate that the *Ver-* in *Vermentino* might originate from the Latin word for "green," *viridis*.

VERMOUTH • People have been flavoring wine for millennia and one of the flavorings used was an herb called wormwood. In the 16th century, the German version of wormwood, wermouth, was marketed as a medicinal wine. By 1806, the word had arrived in English as *vermouth*. The scientific Latin name of wormwood is *Artemisia absinthium*. A far more alcoholic beverage called *absinthe*, also made with wormwood, became popular during the latter part of the 19th century. Reports of psychoactive effects beyond those of alcohol contributed to the widespread (but not universal) banning of absinthe in the early 20th century. The etymology of *absinthe* is traced by reliable sources through Latin to a Greek word, *apsinthion*. Beyond that, the etymology becomes speculative, suggesting that *a* means "not" and *psinthos* means "enjoyable." Such a "not enjoyable" meaning might be consistent with wormwood's bitter taste and is comparable to a Sanskrit word, *ashiva*, meaning "unpleasant."

VERTICAL • A "vertical tasting" is a wine-tasting event where different vintages of the same wine are compared. The reason the word *vertical* means "up and down" has to do with the hair on the human head. *Vertical* more accurately refers to a line passing through the vertex. In English, *vertex* means "top," because in Latin *vertex* meant "whirlpool" and the hair on the human head forms a whorl. That whorl is nominally on the top of the head, hence *vertex* grew to mean "the highest point."

VIDAL • This grape type is valued in Canada and New York State, among other places, for its ability to survive cold winters. It is named after J. Vidal, a director during the early 20th century of a viticultural institute in France known as Institut viticoles Fougerat, Monsieur Fougerat having been a pharmacist whose large estate became the institute. Remembered outside of France for the grape type, Monsieur Vidal is less well remembered at home, since the grape that bore his name has since been rechristened *Sélect* in France.

VIOGNIER • An increasingly popular grape over the past few decades, its French name is cited as early as 1781 and has been speculated to have been applied as an analogy to *viorne*, which is a French name for clematis. *Clematis* in turn is named for its vine-like growth; it comes from the Greek root *klema*, meaning "twig" or "branch of a vine," which is also an ancient relative of the word *clone*.

VINDALOO • "What business," you might ask, "does the name of an especially spicy Indian dish have among the pages of a book dedicated to wine words?" The answer is there in the word itself. *Vindaloo* isn't actually an Indian word, but a word originating in Portuguese. The literal translation is "wine of garlic," since *alho* is Portuguese for "garlic." Yet the *vin* in *vindaloo* isn't actually wine at all; recipes for vindaloo call for vinegar.

VINE • Our English word *vine* appeared in the written record about 700 years ago from a much older French source and from Latin before that. From our modern perspective, vines represent a wide range of plants, from ivy to wisteria. From this perspective, grapevines represent only one example out of many plants that take this form. But looking back at the source of the word *vine*, it becomes clear that instead of grapes growing out of vines, *vine* as a word grew out of grapes. The modern French word for "wine" is *vin*, so it takes little imagination to see that a *vine* got its name from the product it produced.

VINEGAR • Winemakers over the centuries have been careful to seal their wine containers, because alcohol in wine exposed to air becomes acetic acid. When alcohol becomes acetic acid, the wine tastes sour; hence, the word *vinegar* literally means "sour wine" in French. The suffix *aigre*, "sour," comes from the Latin *acer*. It in turn is connected to an Indo-European word, *ak*, meaning "sharp," which also gives English *acrid*. The *acetic* in *acetic acid* represents *acetum*, the Latin word for "vinegar," and both *acetic* and *acid* trace back to that same Indo-European ancestor word.

VINEYARD • Unlike so many wine-related "v" words, such as *vinegar*, *vintage*, and *vintner*, the word *vineyard* did not come to English from the French word for "wine," *vin*. Instead, in Old English, the word had been *wineyard* and had come across the English Channel with the Anglo-Saxons and their

Germanic tongues. The first English citation for *wineyard* occurred around the year 888, but by 1340 the emphasis had shifted to the plant in the yard instead of the beverage it produced. The word *yard* continues back through its Germanic roots to Indo-European origins in the word *gher,* meaning "to enclose." *Yard* grew by parallel routes to also give us the words *garden* and the *-ard* part of *orchard.* The French word for "vineyard" is *vignoble,* which evolved from the Vulgar Latin *vinoporus.* The Romans borrowed half of this word from the Greek word *ampelophoros. Ampelos* was yet another Greek word for "wine" and *phoros* meant "carrier," so *ampelophoros* meant "wine bearing."

VINIFERA • When people talk of *vinifera grapes* or *vinifera varieties,* they are using shorthand for *Vitis vinifera,* the Latin name given to European grapevines by Carl Linnaeus in the 1750s. Linnaeus is the guy we can blame for everything having a Latin name, like people being *Homo sapiens* and dogs being *Canis lupus familiaris. Vitis vinifera* are vines that give grapes that make good wine (potentially). The word *vitis* was a legitimate Classical Latin word meaning "vine." Linnaeus made up *vinifera* because its Latin components meant "wine producing." *Ferre* meant "to bear" or "to carry," and that is why an aqui*fer* "bears" water and a field that is *fer*tile "bears" crops. (See **amphora**, p. 9.)

VINTAGE • Although a wine's vintage is the year in which it was grown, and although the English word *age* is right there inside the word *vintage,* the etymology of *vintage* actually has nothing to do with the year of the wine or its age. The Latin word *vindemia* brought together *vinum* (meaning "wine") and *demere* (meaning "to take away" or "to take off"), so it literally meant "wine take off," or the harvesting of the grapes. The Latin *demere* also gave us *redemption,* by which our sins are taken away. Because the roots of *vintage* literally referred to the harvest, and a wine's quality was influenced by its particular year of harvest, by the time of Shakespeare, *vintage*

178

had taken on a meaning of quality. By 250 years ago, about the time of the great lexicographer Samuel Johnson, *vintage* had also taken on a meaning of "calendar year." It was 1928 when a car was first referred to as *vintage*; in that case, it was a Buick.

VINTNER • The first English report of this French word comes to us from 1297, in an account of a robbery of a wine shop. At first a *vinter*, the professional title of a wine merchant changed to *vintner* by the 15th century. Vintners were more than common merchants. Wine was important enough to the wealthy in England that vintners represented men of great influence. Vintners were repeatedly mayors of London and their trade association was one of only a dozen operating with a royal license. They were wine importers and retailers, not winegrowers. Although wine was grown in England, the quantities and qualities were so inferior to those imported from continental Europe that English doesn't even have a word for this profession. That's not quite true; there is *vigneron*, but it still clearly shows its French heritage and certainly never populated mansions in the classier neighborhoods of London. Instead, now that actual wine production is big business in countries that speak English, the word *vintner* has taken on the meaning of "grower" or "producer" in North America. This leaves *vigneron* standing quayside, blinking in its beret even though it actually stepped off the gangplank and into the English language in 1456.

VITUS • The Latin word for *vine* was *vitis*. That gives us our English word *viticulture*, which is what people who tend vineyards are practicing: the cultivation of vines. There is some debate as to exactly how closely the roots of the Latin word for "wine," *vinum*, intertwines with *vitis*, but *vitis* traces its etymological heritage to words with meanings of "twine" and "wind," for the obvious reason that vines extend tendrils that wind around whatever will support them in their climb to the nourishing sun. Before modern vineyard methods organized vines into straight rows trained along wires or tied to stakes, vines were grown in orchards and trained up trees. Ultimately, the wild cousins of domesticated vines evolved in the company of the trees that they climbed, and that is why wild grapevines are occasionally called *Vitis sylvestra*, *sylvestra* denoting "of the forest"; Silvanus was the Roman god of woodlands.

W

WHITE • Although red wine color ranges from pink to purple to brown, it is evident to any wine drinker why red wine is called *red wine*. White wine is not and never should be the color of milk or snow. Yet the clear, usually light yellow liquid that we call *white wine* is called "white" in other languages too: *bianco* in Italian; *blanc* in French; *blanco* in Spanish; *branco* in Portugese; *leuko* in Greek; *weiß* or *weiss* in German. In Old English, *white* had been *hwit* and, as is made clear by this little list, English got the word from Germanic sources. The Indo-European root *kweit* that led to the Germanic source also ultimately produced our English word *wheat*, named for the color of the flour it produces. *The Oxford English Dictionary* cites 1300 as the first appearance of *win hwit*, but we can be certain that in this case the term had long been used to describe non-red wine.

WINE • Because there is considerable interest in wine and wine history, there has been considerable time given to exploring the etymology of the word *wine*. In addition to illuminating the wanderings of this word through time, these explorations illustrate two general aspects of the study of word histories. One relates to human nature, the other to the imprecision of etymology. *Wine* demonstrates what it is about a word that makes people keep using it. Its attributes not only promote its longevity but also its consistency of meaning. These are the qualities of something very basic to human experience. When absolutely everyone knows what you mean when you say a word, there is a greater chance that the word will survive into the next generation. Because people love to point out the errors of others, such commonly known words have a hard time changing their meaning or pronunciation. Technology and lifestyle come into it; the words *fax* and *modem* will get left behind as *scoggan* already has (it was something very useful to do with the valves of a steam engine).

But people have been drinking the fermented juice of grapes for many thousands of years, and the basics of where that beverage comes from and what it does to the drinker have not changed. That is why the word *wine* has changed so little over thousands of years and across numerous different languages. The imprecision of etymology as a science is displayed in the fact that although there are lots of clues as to the great antiquity of the word *wine*, it has proven impossible to establish a rock-solid timeline of its progress, linguistic inter-relation, and parentage. The beverage was too alluring to wait for the French of the Norman Conquest to bring the word *wine* to English. Although we get *wine* from Latin, the word was already part of the vocabulary of the Anglo-Saxons when they began their takeover of England (nominally in the year 449). So *win* was part of Old English from the start, with the first citations in *Beowulf* around the year 800. But this Germanic linguistic parentage was evidently reluctant. Although Germanic peoples had coexisted, traded, and fought with Romans for centuries, Germanic traditions leaned toward beer not wine. It is thought that Celtic peoples also sharing Europe with Latin speakers learned to appreciate wine (and its name), and that Germanic drinkers subsequently learned from Celts. As with roads, all these word roots lead to Rome and the Latin *vinum*. Yet leading out of Rome back to even earlier etymologies, the map is not so clear. There on distant hills we can see the Greek *oinos* but don't quite know how to get to it. Over the horizon we hear the far-away Arabic *wain*, Hebrew *yayin*, and Assyrian *inn* claiming that wine's parentage likely didn't come from Indo-European yet must be as ancient as that of any word.

X, Y & Z

XAREL-LO • This grape variety is used in Spain for sparkling wines. A claim is made that the name is from the Italian *chiarello*, said to mean "claret," but this is uncertain.

XINOMAVRO • The name of this Greek variety of grape means "acid black," based first on the high degree of acidity it displays and second on its dark color. (See **oxidation**, p. 130.)

XYNISTERI • This grape variety popular in Cyprus takes its name from Greek and was first cited by a Professor Mouillefert in 1893 in a document entitled *Rapport sur une mission viticole à l'île de Chypre*.

YARRA VALLEY • This Australian wine region is named for the Yarra River, which officially gained its name during an 1835 survey of the area. John Helder Wedge evidently considered several Aboriginal names for the river and chose *yarra* because he thought *yarra-yarra* meant "waterfall." He was only slightly off; it's *yarram-yarram* that means "waterfall." *Yarra* means "red gum tree" but could possibly also mean "running water," which gives some etymological consolation. Previously, in 1803, James Flemming had called the river the Freshwater River.

YEAST • Yeast is a single-celled organism that makes bread rise and wine or beer ferment. But no one knew that when the word was first used. Instead, people saw their grape juice mysteriously begin to froth, and a kind of scum accumulate among the bubbles as well as collect at the bottom of the container when the frothing was done. The Indo-European word *jes* or *yes* meant "boil," "foam," or "froth." Via Germanic it got into Old English as *gest* with a meaning of "dregs." It was Louis Pasteur in 1857 who figured out that it was actually the little bitty critters that made up the scum and dregs that were doing the heavy lifting by turning sugar into alcohol and, in so doing, burping out the carbon dioxide that caused all that froth.

ZINFANDEL • The origin of the name of this grape type is uncertain. The earliest records of the name appear in 1830 in Long Island, New York. It wasn't until the 1850s that it arrived in California. The grape type itself is much older and is thought to have been exported to North America from Austria, where in turn it had earlier been imported it from Croatia. Merriam-Webster online indicates that *Zinfandel* is likely an alteration of an outdated Hungarian word, *tzinifändli* or *czirifandli*, which in turn may have been modeled on the name of a white grape called *Zierfandler* in German. Confusingly, another theory is offered by *The Merriam-Webster Unabridged Dictionary*, which suggests the etymology may be from an unidentified European place name.

Index

Index entries in bold represent headwords.

189